a MESSAGE to BLACK AMERICA

MOTIVATING YOUNG, INNER-CITY BLACK MEN to EXCELLENCE

By James A. Hudson

All rights reserved. No part of this publication may be reproduced, stored in a retrieval system, or transmitted, in any form or by any means, electronic, mechanical, photocopying, recording, or otherwise, without the prior written consent of the author.

Copyright © 2017 by James A. Hudson
All rights reserved.

GREEN IVY
PUBLISHING

Green Ivy Publishing
1 Lincoln Centre
18W140 Butterfield Road
Suite 1500
Oakbrook Terrace IL 60181-4843
www.greenivybooks.com

A Message to Black America/James A. Hudson
ISBN: 978-1-946775-48-1
Ebook: 978-1-946775-49-8

A Message to Black America

© 2017 by James A. Hudson

A message to black America, motivating young, inner-city black men into productive citizens, is a course of instructions designed and written to mobilize young, inner-city black men who are lagging behind, to help them lift themselves up by their bootstraps through education, training, and discipline. These instructions also bring to light the importance of honesty, the consequences of crime and violence, and the proper manner in which to interact with the police.

Heaven knows far too many young, inner-city black men have lost their lives in confrontations with law enforcement personnel. And so, the information presented herein will motivate those who are at the lower economic level in black America to rise up.

All rights reserved. No part of this book may be reproduced without consent from the Author, James Augustus Hudson.

Table of Contents

A Message to Black America		III
Introduction		VI
Acknowledgment		XI
Chapter One	The Plight of Young, Black American Men	1
Chapter Two	Good Success Begins with an Education	10
Chapter Three	A Message to Black America	23
Chapter Four	Many Young Black Men Receive No Support	43
Chapter Five	Black People in the Caribbean and Latin America	56
Chapter Six	The Need for Positive Mentors	70
Chapter Seven	Let's Lift Ourselves up by the Bootstraps	80
Chapter Eight	European and Mexican Negroes' Connection	90
Chapter Nine	You Should Stay Away from Bad Influence	100
Conclusion		112
Appendix		114
About the Author		117

Introduction

    A Message to Black America is a course of instructions designed and written to bring, among other things, motivational assistance to young, inner-city black men who are lagging behind others. And so, this book is written to bring a better way of living to the attention of those who are engaged in a life of crime and violence. The fact is that young, inner-city black men should not seek only to get by from day to day but to strive and prosper. The steps necessary to achieve these objectives are laid out in this book.

    In addition to the above, the problems of conflict and clashes with law enforcement personnel that often result in young blacks losing their lives are also discussed. The ways in which one should conduct oneself with the police are clearly brought to light in the book as well. And so, I have an important message for the black American people, which should not be taken lightly. Everyone in black American society should pay particular attention to the *message*, not necessarily to the messenger. It is a sad fact that many of our young black men are under constant attacks from every side. The question is, why is it that so many of our young black men are finding themselves in so much trouble, especially those in the inner cities and at the poverty line? The reasons behind this and the solutions to these problems can be found in this book.

Introduction

Please note that we are presenting the reader with information that will be useful to young inner city black men, and others, at the lower socio economic level and those who are below it. As a result, it's important to bring to the attention the truth—and nothing but the truth. As such, the information in the book is not intended to be offensive to anyone! The fact is that those who are lagging behind are in need of a strong dose of truth. Therefore, I intend to bring the truth to light no matter what!

Young black men are being slaughtered all over this nation, and it's time to put an end to this. If this is allowed to continuing, then the black race in this country is in danger of going extinct. As a result, I firmly believe that they must be taught the appropriate manner in which to conduct themselves in order to prevent such ongoing tragedies. Many of these young men are dying at the hands of their own kind—black on black crime and violence—while others are losing their lives at the hands of the police. In addition, many young black men are losing their lives at the hands of other people such as the likes of one George Zimmerman.

You probably remember Trayvon Martin? For those of you who aren't aware of the matter, Trayvon Martin was the unarmed black teen who was gunned down in the state of Florida by Zimmerman. Although the teen was unarmed, Zimmerman was found not guilty. When will this slaughtering of young black men ever end? In order to combat this situation, the path has been carefully laid out in this book for young black men to follow. But beforehand, we must educate them to be upright citizens. To live lives that should be above reproach. These are some of our objectives here in *A Message to Black America*.

By the way, have you noticed that the penal institutions across this nation are filled to capacity with a disproportionate amount of our young black men? Question: What is the reason behind this? Well, the answer is simple: lack of direction, lack of marketable skills, and rampant unemployment among young black men. These young men aren't being guided in the right and proper direction. In many if not all instances, those in the inner cities and in improvised households are deprived of a male role model or guardian in the home. A father figure is simply not present. They are often out of the picture for one reason or another. And alas, their young male offspring are channeled in

Introduction

the wrong direction.

In any case, before we continue, however, please allow me to set the record straight. The facts presented above are in no way applicable across the board. In other words, not all young black men in this country are deprived of a father figure, living in poverty, or living below the poverty line! And they aren't all committing crimes and violence either. As a result: The message to black America is applicable, for the most part, to young, inner-city black men at the poverty line and below it, young blacks who are caught up in crime and violence, those who have no sense of direction, and those who are clashing with the police.

These young blacks should understand that the police have the authority to maim them or even take their lives! Any physical confrontations or clashes with the police most often end to their advantage. As a result, parents or guardians should teach their children to obey the instructions of the police and to not get into any physical confrontation whatsoever with them since it could well end in a tragic situation for them, as they often do.

And so, this book is designed and written to motivate young black men and women to excellence. I believe that wealthy and middle-class blacks have a moral and ethical responsibility to their fellow black people. They should lend a helping hand to those who are lacking, lagging behind, and failing to make substantial progress in a positive light. We have addressed these issues in the appropriate chapters in this book!

Please note that it should never be forgotten that black American society, just like any other civil society, is divided into three distinct categories. Thus, there are the rich, the middle class, and those at the lower socioeconomic level. Those who are privileged to be in the top category may or may not have much to worry about in terms of poverty, social issues, and unemployment. These are some of the people who should be mentoring young, inner-city blacks who are lagging behind and in need of mentoring!

On the other hand, those in the middle-class bracket may have more to worry about, the reason being that statistics have shown that the American middle class is vanishing at an alarming rate. These middle-class people are vanishing, and soon, there

Introduction

will be none. If this is the case, unfortunately, vanishing middle-class Americans will spiral down to the lower level of the socioeconomic ladder.

And frankly, this scenario is distressing to consider for everyone concerned.

It should be noted, therefore, that if—God forbid—the middle class so happens to be melted downward, they will revert back to the lower level of the spectrum. The phenomena will take place regardless of race, color, or ethnic origin.

On the other hand, those in the upper echelons of society may not have much to worry about in terms of taking care of financial obligations. They are living "high on the hog," as they say. Well, there is not much that we can say about these people except what we have already said: They have a moral responsible to assist their fellow blacks who are at the lower end of the economic and social spectrum. This doesn't necessarily mean handing out financial assistance. No, there are many ways in which they can assist. And in this book, we have presented the manners in which they can help.

It is a fact that the vast majority of blacks in this country aren't rich. The question is, why is this the case? Why is it that the vast majority of the people whose ancestors provided free labor to make this nation a wealthy nation is still at the bottom of the economic and social ladder? Why it is that the vast majority of these people aren't experiencing the American dream? The answer to the question is that they aren't prepared. Are there any blacks in Silicon Valley? I may stand to be corrected, but I cannot say for sure that I have seen any. And this is no credit to the black race in America.

And so, the duty that lies ahead is to instill the fact that blacks at the lower level should be prepared. They should prepare themselves by investing in the future. **They should educate themselves, invest positively in the future, and stop being victims of circumstances.**

It should further be noted that black athletic stars, rock stars, and those in comedy do have their place in this and any in society. However, why not invest and excel in intellectual endeavors!?

Introduction

This is what I am talking about when I mention the fact that there aren't enough blacks making important contributions to science and technology here in this country.

And so, the time has come for this to change once and for all. And I, James Hudson, am spearheading the charge to empower the neglected! This can be achieved through the plan laid out in **A Message to Black America: Motivating Young, Inner-City Black Men to Excellence**.

I would like my readers to be aware of the fact that strong doses of narcotics will not eliminate a bad situation! In fact, they will make it even worse. You see, a sound and alert mind will accomplish much as opposed to a mind that is messed up by the influence of illegal substances! In all probability, a mind under such influence is heading for complete disaster. We have read about these things quite frequently—tragedies in the streets, in the home, and at the workplace. I firmly believe that if one cannot face the world without "being high," there is a problem indeed. We motivate young blacks to stay away from narcotics, and we reveal the terrible consequences as it relates to the tragedy of abuse and dependence on controlled substances.

Please note that the black population in this country is approximately 42 million people, (13%) based on the current population of 350,000,000 people in this country. Blacks therefore, must progress financially, socially and politically and be on parity with its white counterparts.

It's my duty, therefore, to intervene and make things right so that this objective will be realized. Please read this book, tell your friends, relatives, and neighbor so that the process of advancing "the black cause" can begin at once.

Therefore, it's a pleasure for me to present to you valuable and important information in this book, *A Message to Black America: Motivating Young, Inner-City Black Men to Excellence*, by James A. Hudson.

Acknowledgment

I acknowledge the work and death, the deduction, and the sacrifice made by the ancestors of the black American people in terms of the development and advancement of the United States. However, notwithstanding the contributions these people's ancestors made to this nation, the vast majority of black Americans aren't realizing the fruits of the labors of their ancestors. And so, we are turning the spotlight on the failure of the government of the United States for not providing the necessary assistance to black Americans people in a positive and constructive manner.

We are aware, however, that a tiny minority of black people in this country have managed to gain fame and fortune. Nevertheless, the vast majority of blacks are still at the poverty line, and many are well below it.

The black American people should have long ago come of age in terms of economic stability and prosperity. But this is not the case. Blacks who are lagging behind, therefore, must prepare themselves to take full advantage of every opportunity in this society. This should be done with the help of federal, state, and county governments. We cannot overlook corporate America; they have a duty and responsibility in this process. They should step up to the plate and help provide the necessary assistance to young black men. Corporate America should assist in the process. Big businesses can offer technical training, embark on apprenticeship programs, and offer other assistance of this natures.

Acknowledgment

The fact is that the burning desire for a vast number of American black people—those at the lower economic level—is to move forward and gain economic parity with their European American counterparts. The truth is, however, that many blacks, especially those within the inner cities, aren't prepared in the first place.

And so, the purpose of the book is threefold:

1. To lay down guidelines that blacks at the lower level should follow
2. To stimulate them into becoming productive citizens in their society
3. To instill the fact that the road to prosperity is through education and training—training in terms of acquiring at least one marketable skill!

Many at the lower economic level in the black communities, those who are lagging behind in terms of education and skills, are encouraged and motivated. They are encouraged to educate themselves and invest positively in their futures. And above all, they are encouraged to stop accepting themselves as being victims of circumstances.

It is a fact that the federal government owed the black American people an education. I am referring to free education, all the way to the institution of higher learning. One may argue that this statement is ridiculous.

Our government gives billions of the Americans taxpayer dollars to foreign nations annually. Is not *this* being ridiculous? Yes, it is! And we will come back to this in the appropriate chapters.

It should never be forgotten that these people's ancestors weren't permitted to get an education. Well, let's not reopen old wounds here. What I am referring to is the fact that the US government should see to it that these people—those disenfranchised in the inner cities across America—should attend school all the way to college and above, at the taxpayer's expense. In addition, they should be trained in science and technology. This alone would reduce the arrival of expatriates coming to this

Acknowledgment

country and taking existing jobs in the areas of high technologies.

Black American society will not come of age, economically, unless and until all members of that society are educated and trained in all fields of science and technology! And so, this book, *A Message to Black America*, is developed and written to bring awareness with a view that they—blacks and the mainstream society at large—will see the light and act accordingly.

You are aware that many young blacks often excel in sports and in music. What you probably aren't aware of is that many young blacks—again, those at the poverty level—often fail to graduate from school. The dropout rate for black students is many times that of white students. If this trend is allowed to continue, what will be the future of black America? Achievements in sports and music are admirable. And those in these businesses should be commended for their contributions to society at large, their race, and themselves. Nevertheless, black America should expect more from young black men.

The question is, how can we expect more when we haven't invested in them?

This society needs to turn out more black scientists, black engineers, black physicians, etc. When these goals are achieved, then the race will be credited for making substantial contributions to society and to the black race in particular.

In terms of social integration of black people in American society, this is moving in the right direction but at a snail's pace. Much too slowly! This process, therefore, must gain rapid momentum in order to bring every black American up to par with their white counterparts. And, as already mentioned, for these things to be achieved, those at the lower end of the economic spectrum—which comprises the vast majority in black America—must be brought up to parity.

But first, we must eradicate the ills that beset many black communes across the nation: poverty, illiteracy, unemployment, and low morale. One can understand the gigantic task that's ahead in terms of bringing assistance to those who are in these desperate situations.

In any case, before concluding this acknowledgment, we

Acknowledgment

should recognize, and we do recognize, the blacks in this country who have made substantial gains. Gains in areas of science, engineering, medicine, law, etc. Nevertheless, we need more of them! These people are a tiny minority of the black population. We are desperately in needs of more of these high achievers. In fact, these people are proving that if given the opportunities, black people are capable of achieving greatness! In any case, good luck to our professional friends in black American society. And may they strive and prosper for many years to come!

Chapter One
The Plight of Young, Black American Men

Black America needs to pool its resources in order to prevent our young black men from going on the endangered species list. It's clear that there is a problem in connection with the tragedies facing this group of people. Frankly, I am embarrassed when confronted with the reality facing young black men, especially those in the inner cities and at the poverty line across the nation. Their actions, plights, and legal entanglements are blemishing everyone, especially blacks who are making positive contributions to American society.

The question is, what is the reason behind the meltdown dynamic that is affecting our people, especially young men between seven and twenty-seven years of age? We will look into this in a moment and offer suggestions for the cure. Every problem has its solution. And the problem facing young black men is no exception. The cures are there! And we will present them in the book.

Now, since this topic is current—the killing of unarmed blacks by the police and others—let's look into the matter so that you will understand the dynamic and the magnitude in connection with the problem facing America in general and black America in particular.

The Plight of Young, Black American Men

This certainly brings us to the city of Ferguson in the State of Missouri, where a young black man lost his life to the hands of the police. Now, whether or not the killing was justified or not justified, is beside the point. The point is that the boy is dead. And this is not an isolated incident. This happens all the time, too frequently, all across this nation! In addition, the killing of blacks by other blacks is another cause for concerns, and furthermore, so is the killing of blacks by citizens and non-citizens alike. An example would be the killing of Trayvon Martin in the state of Florida by one George Zimmerman. The point is that the black communities are losing their people at an alarming rate, and this cannot be allowed to continue. Black people must make a concerted effort to put an end to the destruction of their people. We cannot allow these things to continue. We must come up with a solution to prevent the slaughtering of the next generation of black people.

The following is a true story. A German friend said to me the other day, "James, why it is that young black men in this country are getting themselves into so much trouble, even with the police? Is this because they are dumb?"

He went on to say, "Why are they confronting the police, who are armed and can take their lives?"

I pondered his questions for a while then let him know that the problems often applied to poor, inner-city kids who are misguided.

What general impression is given to everyone in this country and people around the world about black people in America? Not good. Frankly, the image is devastating to everyone. This must change. And the time to begin the process is now. You who are reading this book have a part to play in turning this around! If meaningful changes are to take place, every black person has their part to play. We cannot wait for white America to do the work we should be doing for ourselves. However, we welcome any and all assistance that our white brothers and sisters are able to render. In fact, those of you who are wealthy and those of you who are middle-class are welcome to participate. Please do not worry about anything. Remember, "Strength for your labor the Lord will provide."

The Plight of Young, Black American Men

The problem of isolation, resentment, and scorn for the less fortunate is something that one should guard against! Remember, whatever one can do to help another fellow man would be welcomed by Providence. There are people, though, who would rather leave their wealth to their pets than to another human or groups of impoverished people. To those people, I say, may their immortal souls rest in peace. There are also others who will make great contributions to their favorite political party rather than build affordable houses for the homeless and sending inner city impoverished kids to community college to learn a skill. It's a fact, many of the wealthy people in Hollywood, Silicon Valley, Wall Street, etc., would rather donate millions of dollars to their favorite political party rather than helping inner city kids at the poverty line. These are some of the people who make up the population of the American society!

In addition to all the above, there are wealthy citizens who have donated hundreds of millions to National monuments, to the preservations of rare documents, etc., rather than donate money to help inner-city blacks who are in poverty. Well, it's written, "the fool and his money will soon depart." In other words, the money will do no good to them after they are dead. As such, they should help the needy in order to leave this world with a clean conscience.

In terms of crime and violence, it should be noted that when a black person does something wrong, the entire race is affected negatively. On the other hand, when one of us blacks makes significant progress, all blacks are proud. This is the reason that able blacks must come to the assistance of inner-city blacks at the poverty line and helping them to rise. This will be winning, win situation for everyone!

In fact, we should help those at the bottom up the ladder of success. That is, those who are rich and famous, those in the middleclass and black intellectuals should come to the assistance of inner cities blacks who are left behind. Other minority races have done similar things for their people. For example, people of Israeli descent are still doing this. Those who are wealthy are still helping their people to rise. And today, they are a wealthy people. This is also true for Asian people in this country. This is the primary purpose of the "Asian Banks." The Asian Bank is

The Plight of Young, Black American Men

established to assist people of Asian descent here in the United States. On the contrary, where is the black American bank in black American society? There *are* rich and famous black Americans as mentioned. Yet, where is the bank that they formed in order to help black business people, and those who are aspired to go in business? Can't they get together and form black business banks to promote and give low interest loan to black business people and those who are aspired to go into business of their own? This would be a dynamic situation for the black America people and for America in general.

Well, there are all kinds of grim statistics bringing to light the plight of young black men. One of these is the statistic in terms of the prison population across the United States. And frankly, this is not good news. In fact, the report places young blacks as the majority in the penal institutions across the nation.

The fact is, it would be mistaken to place all young black men in one category. No, a distinction should be clearly drawn! There are young black men who are doing well from an economic, intellectual and social stand point. Remember, blacks are divided into three categories as mentioned. And frankly, there are inner cities blacks who are not engaged in crime and violence either! This should never be forgotten! Poverty does not necessarily equate to lawlessness, crime, violence and other nefarious activities. In other word, it doesn't mean that because a person is in poverty that person is involved in crime, violence, and other nefarious activities, far from it!

However, there is certainly a problem that is in need of attention—not only attention but also correction. We must take a stand to have our young black men who are engage in crime sees and desist from this and be honest and upright citizens. And the problem concerns to all of us who are black people from coast to coast! If we unite and pool our resources, we will stand and turn the tide against poverty and illiteracy. On the contrary, if blacks continue to divide themselves into subgroups, the outcome will not be good! What is the reason behind this in the first place? The majority of blacks in the cities who are improvised are in need of assistance. And they need your help now.

Our duty is clear. We must develop workable strategies in

The Plight of Young, Black American Men

order to combat the evil facing our young black men who are improvised. We are losing too many of them. It is said that young black men are either in jail or they are dead. Well, the fact is that this is not the case as mentioned! Many aren't doing well, but they are there wafting for things to change in their favor. And our duty is to prevent them from extinction by give them the education, training and marketable skills they desperately deserve.

Am I making sense here? These people are at the lower level and should be lifted up.

Earlier, I mentioned the killing of a young black man in Ferguson, Missouri. The untimely death of this young man ignited all sorts of problems in Ferguson and around the country. The question is, could this boy have been taken down by the police alive? This was possible. Yes, it's possible to shoot a man and wound him without killing him. This happens all the time. The police are aware of this. They know the manner in which to shoot and wound an individual without taking a life! It should be clear to the police, and everyone, that killing an unarmed black man will bring about serious backlash. And it is detrimental to race relations when a white police officer kills an unarmed black person.

By the way, have you ever noticed that any time racial harmony seems to be making progress in a positive direction, then comes a setback that cancels out the momentum completely? And heavens know, it often takes a long time before racial harmony is once again restored somewhat between the two major racial groups in this country. The police should be mindful of this fact. Or is it that they aren't concerned? You and everyone else saw what happened in Ferguson, Missouri in 2016. The killing of this unarmed black teen set off a firestorm. The police chief resigned. A municipal court judge resigned. A city manager resigned. The list goes on and on. I believe that these things could have been avoided. Well, where there is no vision, the people are sure to perish.

And so, an ounce of prevention is far better that a pound of cure. This applies equally across the board. Before taking a person's life, the police should weigh all options. Remember, remorse will not bring back a life that is deceased. Remember

The Plight of Young, Black American Men

further, having someone else's blood on one's hands should be the last thing that a man should be willing to live with for the rest of his life. Yes, criminals and others often take the lives of innocent people. However, many of them cannot live with themselves with the passage of time. And some, often, take their own lives!

What can be done to prevent our young black men from colliding with the police? This is the question that you and I should be concerned about. We should not only be concerned, but we should offer constructive suggestions in order to prevent this trend from happening in the first place. As a result, I decided that I would write this book to give specific instructions in this matter. Thus, specifics instructions on the matter are given in this book.

In any event, to correct this and other problems facing young black men, we should start by examining the home environment. The home environment—or the lack of a proper home environment—is usually the root of ongoing problems related to misguided, young black men. The absence of a father figure and neglect by motherhood are, indeed, contributing factors to the stagnation of black America.

This is a persistent plight that's affecting poor, inner-city neighborhoods. Young, immature girls are giving birth to children they cannot adequately care for; young, immature males aren't in the financial standing to provide for their children. These are all major reasons for the decay. And so, the breaking down of the family structure in black communities is the culprit behind most if not all of the evil in terms of young black men going astray.

What part does government play in the equation? Well, another contributing factor is that young mothers aren't qualified to receive social assistance when a male figure is present in the house. As a result, many fathers often disappear from the scene in order for females to receive the necessary social assistance. Is this a willful act to ruined blacks in this country? Black families have been ruined to the point of no return. And this is true for those in impoverished communities. These people are in need of training to help themselves. That is, education, disciplinary training and yes, marketable skills.

The Plight of Young, Black American Men

Government policy in terms of social service issues and other issues is a contributing factor behind the ills of the black American society at the lower level in America. In addition, as far as the justice system is concerned, the deck seems to be stacked against black men. They are more likely to be sentenced for the possession of marijuana than their white counterparts. And, being convicted unfortunately, many are excluded from well-paying jobs. Worse, many of these people are not qualified for student loans in order to attend college etc. And so, the revolving door, in and out of prison, has become the way of life for thousands of inner city young black men. These people deserve better. And what is the society doing about this?

Remember our earlier discussion relative to the problem of young black men going astray? Please note that the problem often applies to those at the lower economic level in the inner city of the black society; this problem is not widespread across the board. In other words, upper and middle-class young black men aren't going astray! Many of these young men are living exemplary lives. People in the categories mentioned are somewhat sheltered from poverty. As such, young black men in these categories aren't running around crazily committing crimes, confronting the police, and bringing shame and disgrace to black society.

However, as you and everyone else is fully aware, wealthy blacks and those in the middle income brackets are a tiny minority of people in black American society!

I am not going to give a percentage in terms of the amount of rich and middle-class blacks in America. However, they are probably less than five hundred. I stand to be corrected on the numbers of those in the category mentioned. The important thing here is that these people should pool their resources and help their fellow blacks at the poverty line, not necessarily from a financial standpoint but from a mentoring point of view.

It should be noted that it is not only young black men who are plagued with ongoing problems. Young black women at the lower economic level aren't exempt either. As a result, specific instructions are given to them in this book.

The Plight of Young, Black American Men

Inner-city poverty doesn't discriminate. However, girls and women have their own unique and particular problems. Many of them have dropped out of school due to unplanned pregnancies among other things. And so, they stay home in order to care for their child or children, etc. It's interesting to note that many of the young girls who drop out of school and miss out on an education often end up in poverty. And this cycle will probably be repeated in the next generation.

It should be noted that quality parents will, in all probability, raise quality children and not the other way around. Because of this dynamic, I cannot overstress the importance that young girls should be abstinent until they have finished their education and are married. Bringing children into the world unprepared should not be an option! In addition, it takes two parents to raise children. And since the burden of providing for a family is a man's responsibility, he should be in a position to provide for his family.

Indeed, there is work to do. And black America should reinvent itself. In my opinion, there should be an association dedicated to looking out for the interests of blacks at the lower economic level. I am not talking about another civil rights organization. What I am referencing here is an origination designed to instill mentoring to blacks who are in need of mentoring. Let's name this proposed organization the Early Black Education and Mentoring Association. The proposed organization would see that young blacks are brought up in the proper way—attend school, learn discipline, gain a marketable skill or skills, and stay away from the use of drugs and other mind-altering substances.

Discipline should be instilled at an early age. And the proposed organization would be responsible for seeing that this is instituted.

In addition, this organization would teach young black men the appropriate manner in which to interact with law enforcement personnel. In fact, children should be taught not to get into confrontations with anyone. Not in school, not in the home, and not in public places. We will discuss these issues at length in another chapter.

The Plight of Young, Black American Men

One can understand the value of such an organization. In any event, there is valuable information in terms of turning the tide in favor of young black men when we continue in the chapters throughout this book!

Before leaving this chapter, please note: In this chapter, I brought to your attention the plight facing young black men. We discussed current problems and the impact they have on every black person in this country. An example of the killing of an unarmed black youth by the police in Ferguson, Missouri and others were brought to your attention. We came to the conclusion that the failures in many poor, inner-city neighborhoods, as well as government policies, are responsible for much of the decay and many of the problems facing young black men. Young black women who drop out of school and don't get an education are also contributing factors in the problems. As a result, the need for an organization for the cause of young black Americans was brought to your attention.

The fact is that young, inner-city blacks are in need of intellectuals as role models. Although sports and music have their place, blacks are capable of excelling at higher levels. The proposed mentoring organization mentioned would be charged with the responsibility of instilling values and motivating young blacks in positive directions.

In the next chapter, I will bring to light the steps that are necessary for bringing healing and success to young, inner-city blacks in America. Many of you may be in need of remedial steps. This book will point to the direction in this regard!

Since success is the thing everyone aspires to attain, it should be understood that an educated mind is one sure way to success. This is not to say that one cannot attain success without an education. Nevertheless, an educated mind is an intelligent mind as opposed to an uneducated mind. As such, the next chapter will be dedicated to bringing the importance of education to the reader's attention. The steps that are necessary to bring young black men up to par, among other things, are given in the chapter.

Chapter Two
Good Success Begins with an Education

The declining educational system in this country places us below many other nations in terms of students graduating from high school, and there is no end in sight. This is devastating for the future of the United States and for black society in particular. This is unacceptable. What can be done, then, to stimulate the interest of our black students so as to keep them in school until they graduate? Well, we are going to look at this in this chapter.

Before we continue, it should be noted that a good foundation should be laid out at the grammar school level before students are qualified to proceed to the higher level of learning: technical school, community colleges, and above. Early childhood education hopefully will lay a firm foundation. This is where the groundwork is laid for future development! In fact, there are gifted children who will excel without intense early education. This, however, is the exception and not the rule.

For all practical purposes, therefore, our children should progress through the lower level before attempting to attend higher institutions of learning. In my opinion, this is one of the reasons behind the high dropout rate of high school students in America. They weren't properly prepared beforehand. And so, many of them are more frustrated than anything else, and they simply cannot cope with higher-level material. Does this make

Good Success Begins with an Education

any sense to you? I sincerely hope so!

Preparation Is the Key for Young Black Men

You should be cognizant of the fact that education is the master key to success. Without an adequate education, the future, in all likelihood, may not be as bright has it could have been. As a result, one should be educated in primary school and continue to at least the high school level. And there is a good reason behind this!

This is not to say that not attending school will prevent one from making a living. No, but, God forbid, what kind of a living? What kind of a future will one enjoy? There are many out there who never had the good fortune of an education. And many of these people are surviving somehow. Well, surviving is not enough. They should be prospering. Many of these people are struggling in this society. Without being able to read, write, and understand things is truly a disadvantage. My suggestion, then, is that every black person in the inner cities who cannot read should go to school. Some may be in needs of remedial action in order to make maximum use of continued education.

Education is one good way out of the woods—the ghetto, the low places—and out of poverty. All of our young black men and women should be exposed to this refinement. They should learn to think, to use their brains, and to make intelligent decisions. This important element should be instilled at an early age. "This is one way" to gain economic prosperity and a great way to gain respect among peers and others.

Please note that one should understand that *respect* is something that one earns. No one will command respect unless one has earned it. As a result, preparing oneself for the future will certainly command a great deal of respect! How can a young man ever hope to be respected wearing the so called dreadlocks? That is, the head of hair resembling something from the Stone Age. In good faith, no one will make mention to this derogatory attire, but they will certainly shunt those who are engage in this sought of practice. If I were an employer I would not hire young men, nor young girls who are wearing the dreadlock attire!   One

Good Success Begins with an Education

should be well groomed for success.

In terms of education, there are people who aren't able to physically attend school. In this case, the school can come to them. Education is being offered online. All that's required is a computer or some other device that is able to connect to the World Wide Web. This is a positive way to prepare oneself for the future and to stop being a victim of circumstance.

I know that there is a lot of blame to go around. This attitude, however, will not solve any of the problems faced by inner-city blacks. Instead, hard work, preparation, and commitment to excellence will! This lagging behind by many of our black citizens, those at the bottom of the totem pole, are directly or indirectly related to a lack of education, the lack of skills or a trade, and not being able to make wise and prudent decisions!

It should be noted that "skilled craftsmen" earn good salaries. To become a skilled craftsman or woman, technical training is necessary. In addition, one cannot become skilled craftsmen without knowledge of mathematics, physics, etc. Please note that the opportunity for a high school education does exist. And thank Heaven this is currently free of charge. In addition, there are technical schools and community colleges all over. As such, there should be no excuse for blacks in inner-city populations to be lagging behind everyone else. Therefore, the time for action has arrived.

Student loans are available for those who desire to gain higher education in terms of becoming professionals. Regarding this matter, I frankly believe that every young black man and woman whose ancestors provided slave labor to this country should be educated at higher educational institutions at the expense of taxpayers. Yes, I believed that federal, state, and county governments have a responsibility and a duty to educate these people at the taxpayer's expense. This would be a win-win situation for everyone—black America and the United States of America.

Well, one of the troubling things is the position of critics of government involvement in social issues policies. Many of

Good Success Begins with an Education

these people complain about those who are on the receiving end of "entitlement programs." In fact, many critics are in bitter opposition against them. They moan and complain about the little that is being given to the poor and indigents among us. On the other hand, these people aren't complaining about the billions of taxpayer dollars given to foreign governments annually. They are not complaining when it comes to grants being given to foreign governments. Indeed, billions of US taxpayer dollars are being poured into the coffers of many foreign governments on an annual basis. In this case, I will cite three nations in the Middle Eastern regions that are receiving US aid on a constant basis: Pakistan, Afghanistan, and Israel. I firmly believe that these billions of taxpayer dollars should go toward lifting up black America. In fact, if this nation is to remain a superpower, we must educate our people! This includes young men and women at the poverty line in black America.

It is good to help others. Nevertheless, we should help our own people first.

Young black men and women who are in prison should be educated. Many of these people are there because of ignorance in the first place! The government did not see to it that they received an adequate education. In fact, this is directly related to the failure of the government and its policies. These people who are left behind were taught to be dependent rather than to be independent. They were taught "how to eat fish" rather than how to catch fish for themselves. This paralysis is pervasive right across the spectrum. In other words, this paralysis does not affect black America exclusively but also poor whites and Hispanics in the inner cities as well.

The fact is that, as a wealthy, developed nation, we are lacking in many ways. One of the ways in which we are lacking is in the area of educating our people. In fact, America is at the bottom of the barrel when it comes to education. And this is bad news for everyone. Frankly, this cannot be allowed to continue indefinitely.

Many young black men are affected many times over as a result of the declining educational system. Worst of all, many of the people who graduated from the system are functionally

Good Success Begins with an Education

illiterate! This is one of the reasons that these people seem to have no sense of direction. And many have taken out their frustrations on society. As a result, we should set the record straight by telling them exactly what they needed to know. This is the purpose of *A Message to Black America*.

What Young Black Men Should Be Mindful Of

The question of economic viability and success demands a great deal of preparation. That is, preparation from kindergarten, elementary school, college, and above. One should be cognizant of the fact that there are rules and regulations that govern the principles of success. And it should be taught in the home and, frankly, in the public school system.

Unfortunately, this is not the case. We as a society turn out thousands of so-called graduates annually, blacks, whites, and others. And a vast number of graduates aren't able to function competitively. Worse, those who have dropped out of high schools due to frustration are left out and almost always fall through the cracks of society.

This is a major factor behind the disparity in terms of wealth and poverty. There are other reasons for the inequity of wealth distribution. One should remember that success is dependent on one's ability to make significant contributions to society. Flipping burgers, for example, may be honorable; however, it would be far more honorable to be a professional contributing to science, technologies, engineering, etc. We aren't condemning our friends who are providing the hamburger services, but this line of work should be a stepping stone for further advancements. That is a means to an end.

If you happen to be one of those engaged in low-paying jobs, it's time to move up the ladders. You should follow the instructions presented in this book and upgrade yourself ASAP!

I have a message here for the parents and guardians of children. You should see to it that your child stays in school and does not quit until they graduate. They should go through the process determined by the educational system. It may not be adequate. Nevertheless, it's all that is available as the present. In addition to what has been taught in the school, there are

Good Success Begins with an Education

things that you as parent/guardian can teach the child in order to stimulate the mind for success. I have prepared a list consisting of five principles that you should teach child/children. You will not find them in any textbooks!

This is developed exclusively by me to contribute to the well-being of our people. Too many young black men are lost and need to find the way out of poverty, drugs, crime, and violence. I invite you to pleases contemplate the instructions what follow for your benefit and the benefit of your child/children.

The Five Important Principles for Success

1. Go to school and stay in school and do not quit until you have graduated
2. Don't run afoul of the law; be an upright and law-abiding citizen
3. Stay away from any and all forms of mind-altering substance abuse
4. Don't get pregnant or get anyone pregnant until you are married
5. Learn at least one marketable skill for you and your family's future

We will discuss these principles in more detail later. However, you can understand the importance of what we are trying to instill in our younger generation. For the matured mind, they may not need great a deal of clarification. To those who are in need of additional clarification, I will elaborate on these principles and the reasons behind them at the appropriate place in the book.

One thing is for sure. Success doesn't happen by chance or luck. The wise man declared: "There is no such thing as luck." And there seems to be some truth to this proclamation. I firmly believe that preparation for success is the key! And this preparation begins at an early age. It is said by legends that "success promises no man." in other words, no one is guaranteed that one will be rich and famous in this life. As such, one option to combat this is

Good Success Begins with an Education

preparation for the future.

In fact, this believed may be true in the sense when preparation was not made. The fact is to meet with Mr. Success, one must prepare beforehand. The important message that we are sending here is: One should educate oneself. That is, invest positively in the future. And above all, young, inner-city black men should cease and desist considering themselves victims of circumstances. Many consider themselves to be victims, and this is not the case! We will revisit the matter later.

You may have heard the proverb "The Lord helps those who help themselves." Actually, I have a twist to this belief. I say that the Lord helps him who prepares for the future. Indeed, it's all about the future. And without some form of preparation, the future will be virtually hopeless.

Let's examine some interesting black inventors and their contributions to American society. In fact, I will bring only one of many post-Emancipation black inventors to your attention. You may consult the libraries in your city for additional information.

Early Black Inventors

We can learn from the past in order to prepare ourselves and our children for the future. Now, after Reconstruction following the American Civil War, many blacks were engaged in meaningful activities that we admire to this day. Activities that gave us many inventions that are widely in use throughout the United States and the world. One of these early inventors was Granville T. Woods.

Woods, who begin his work around 1885 or 1886, invented many apparatuses ranging from electronics to steam boilers and also the famous air brake system. The fledgling Bell Telephone Company bought Woods's innovations in the field of telephone and telegraphy. On the other hand, the budding General Electric Company bought Woods's electronics inventions. And the Westinghouse Company bought Woods's air brakes business before his death in 1910.

We are in need of people similar to the likes of Woods. Woods wasn't the only black inventor in the post-Emancipation era. There is a long list of them, but I will not bore you by attempting

Good Success Begins with an Education

to present them all in this chapter.

Frankly, the opportunity for higher education for blacks today is greater than that of the post-Reconstruction era. In fact, the opportunities for black people today are greater than they were thirty, twenty, or even just ten years ago. As far as things are concerned today, there is no reason for limitation. The only limitation is the lack of a good education, lack of vision, and the lack of preparation for the future! Today, we have affirmative action legislation and other equal rights acts that guarantee blacks a fair chance. Yet, many in the lower strata aren't doing as well as they should be doing. They are lagging behind, even behind recent immigrants to the United States. Many of our young black men in the inner cities aren't making any progress whosoever, and this is embarrassing.

There is no reason why today's blacks cannot achieve more. Black leaders who are advocating for the rights of blacks—and rightfully so—need to do more! They need to ignite in these people the value of education, self-respect, brotherly love, and honesty.

Maybe I am getting ahead of myself here. Civil rights may not have much to do with motivating young blacks into excellent citizens. This is where the proposed organization that I envisioned would enter into the equation.

In any event, I would like to see a copy of this book in the hands of every black person so that the gospel according to me, James Hudson, can spread across the nation. It is time that the truth is made known, and it appears that the lot has fallen on me to tell it.

Now, the question that I have for you is, what do you think about the code of ethics, the code of conduct, demonstrated by the overwhelming numbers of our young blacks in the cities today? Are you proud of their behavior? These young black men are portraying images that are cause for concerned. And so, let's examine this for a moment with a view of setting the record straight. A neat and pleasant appearance will instill confidence. In fact, people often judged others on their appearances. Therefore, they should dress well, look well, and be pleasing to the eye. Please note that this dreadlocks hairstyle many of our black men are wearing will instill fear and resentments. So for God's sake,

Good Success Begins with an Education

stop it ASAP. Be a shining light for your race and you for all to see.

Embarrassing Image Portrayed by Young Black Men

As a member of the black race, I am deeply offended, if not embarrassed, by the images portrayed by many young blacks in the communities. The dress code, for example, by many in the inner cities leaves much to be desired: oversized pants are hanging down over the hips, exposing the undergarments, and heads are covered in dreadlocks. Where are the parents/guardians of these young men? Don't adults have a moral responsibility to bring guidance? What kind of message are these people sending to the world about blacks in this country?

These are some of the things we should eradicate from among us. The above mentioned, however, is not restricted to young black men alone. In every race, there are characters who are willing to bring down their race, wittingly or unwittingly. And in the black communities, there is no exception.

As members of a minority, we should hold our heads high. High, to gain the necessary respect and to advance the black race to be counted as progressive people. Yes, we should portray dignity, self-respect, and good character—even those who are deemed descendent of slaves. We aren't alone! The Israelite people's ancestors were also slaves. They were enslaved in Egypt for over 400 years until Moses brought them out of slavery. Look at them today. Aren't they progressive people? Yes, they are! Then why can't we, the black race here in America, be like them? Why this lagging behind everyone else? The time has come to cast off this cloak and mask and move ahead. This will not happen without action, and we are counting on you as well.

Now, those who are defaming the black race must rethink their position. The question is, who are those who are supposed to be doing the monitoring and suggesting corrective actions? Where are the black leaders? Isn't it the responsibility of the groups or part of the group to monitor their own? We can't wait until it's too late and our youths are thrown into government corrective institutions. We must act to bring some sense of discipline and dignity to our young people. We must respect ourselves, our race, and our communities before we can hope for others to respect

Good Success Begins with an Education

and help us!

How can we hope to advance and achieve an economic dynamic when we are looked on with eyes of scrutiny, brought about by many young blacks in the inner cities who are failing? The time has come for all black Americans to take a stand, and we should begin without delay. We must be firm in our resolve to turn things around for the benefit of all in the black American society.

This brings us to a few inner-city youths who formed themselves into street gang cults and are raining terror on their communities and their people. They are desecrating themselves, their communities, and their race without realizing it.

Are we to understand that their relatives sided with them in wrongdoings? It is doubtful. And so, it's time that these fellows cleaned up their acts and fell in line. Or else they will only play into the hands of the local police who will not have any mercy on them! In fact, this can be seen across this nation, and frankly it is not pleasant to watch.

Playing the Race Card Unnecessarily Is a Bad Idea

As a naturalized American citizen of Jamaican origin and a member of the black community, I strongly disagree with the position of the overplaying of "the race card" on a regular basis, especially when it is not warranted. Our black American counterparts are apt to play the race card unwarranted, at times to their disadvantage.

Playing the race card when it is justified, in some instances, may be plausible. However, "crying wolf," when there is no wolf is self-defeating and should be discouraged. In other words, it is self-defeating for one to be screaming "racism" when racism wasn't intended in the first place or when no racialism existed.

No one wants to be labeled *a racist, even though they may be racist*. No one wants to be caught in an uncomfortable position to be defending oneself and one's organization against the accusation of **racism, although racism should be exposed for what it truly is**!

The fact is, this stigma is shunned by everyone due to the

Good Success Begins with an Education

"fallout factor" and lasting negative consequence this often generated. No, no—racism is a subject no one wants to debate in this country. People would rather sweep the subject under the rug. This is the very reason that racial problems will not go away anytime in the near or even distant future. Until the matter is discuss and deal with openly and lay to rest once and for all!

It should be noted, then, that due to the fallout factor, as well as the legal implications involved, many American companies, as well as foreign companies doing business in the United States, would rather look for other alternatives. That is, other alternatives in terms of not wanting to do business with black America. And so, you understand the negative consequences the above has on the entire race of people, young black men in particular. These companies would rather do business with other minorities other than blacks.

And so, the shunning factor of not wanting to do business with black America has taken its toll over the years. People are literally afraid, and rightfully so, *of the misconception when things don't go favorably*, and one can understand this dynamic. After all, self-preservation is the key—the key in business, housing, and in the social life of people. Only the demented mind wants to expose himself to potential trouble, real or imaginary, when it comes to the issue of people claiming racial discrimination.

One should be cognizant of the fact that there are other minority groups in this country other than blacks. After all, minority is minority. And other minorities are willing and ready to undercut blacks, as already mentioned. These minorities aren't mindful of, nor do they care about the legacy of the American black people. Their objectives are to forge ahead and make a living for themselves and their connections. And they will do whatever is necessary to prevent "rocking the boat," as they say. And, in fact, these people will not complain about anything. As a result, they will throw a roadblock in the path of blacks, undermining the case of blacks' legacy. In fact, this is currently the case. Other minorities are currently cashing in on the black's legacies. They are competing with blacks for jobs, housing and school etc. And the powers that be would rather invest in other minorities than in the blacks whose ancestor does so much for his country without receiving just reward. You should have a good look on

Good Success Begins with an Education

the Television programs on ABC, CBS, and NBC to determine the truth about this. Those who are hankering those program are almost always minorities. Those at the top recited these people and trine them to carry out these duties. But as far as we are concerned the day of **recompense** will come!

The fact is that other minority groups don't worry about discriminations and bigotry as many blacks do. In fact, they are the last to file discrimination suits against anyone or any organization. As such, this makes these groups of people very attractive to large businesses as well as small business enterprises! In general, these groups of minorities are at an advantage while blacks are at a disadvantage for the most part!

I hope this sheds light on a very important issue facing the black American society. I myself have witnessed the bitterness and revenge resulting from the cry of racial discriminations. I believe that if one believes they have been unfairly treated in any area—whether on the job, in housing, at school, etc.—it would be better to find another alternative. "Cut clean" is an appropriate course of action. Remember, you have an entire race of people to protect. Remember further, whenever a black person does something wrong, it is reflected on the entire black race! Instead, please leave the offender to Providence. The time will come when the offenders will cease offending. And yes, recompense no man evil for evil. Remember, vengeance belongs to God; He will repay them!

In this chapter, we examined the importance of an educated mind. There are many paths to success. However, without a proper educational foundation, one will, in all probability, miss out. In addition, the problem of playing the race card was explained. The way in which many inner-city black youths carry themselves was brought to attention with a view of correction.

In addition, we examined the problem of poor behavior by many young, inner-city black men bringing embarrassment on all of us in black America. Young black people are not making the necessary progress should be making. The fact is that modern blacks can do much better. The achievement of one early black inventor, Granville T. Woods, and his inventions was also presented.

Good Success Begins with an Education

In addition to all the above, young blacks must present a savory image to America and the world. In fact, behavior must be examined and changed. Respect for self, neighbors, and authorities must be maintained. And above all, the mentoring of young, inner-city black men by affluent, intellectual, and professional blacks should take priority.

In the next chapter, we will present the *Message to Black America* with an emphasis on directing young black men in the right and proper direction.

Chapter Three
A Message to Black America

A message to black America is designed and written to bring a strong message mainly to young black men and women in the inner cities across this nation and those at the lower ends of the economic spectrum. As such, this is a course of instructions intended to bring motivational teaching and mentoring to those who are lagging behind.

Many blacks in the inner cities are at an economic disadvantage. Many believe that they are "victims of circumstance." The truth is that they aren't victims of circumstance! This will become clear during our presentations. The question of "disadvantage" is another matter. Yes, many of these people are at a disadvantage! However, they are at a disadvantage because they have failed to qualify themselves in order to take advantage of existing and future opportunities. And we will point them in the right direction for success.

First, it should be made clear that preparation is the key. One cannot hope to go on a long journey without being prepared. For example, if one intended to drive from New York to, let's say, Los Angeles, the first line of thinking would be to plan the driving direction. It may be necessary for one to consult a roadmap for directions beforehand. There is no point in leaving New York not knowing the direction to California. This would be confusing, wouldn't it? Well, similar principles apply to success. One will not

A Message to Black America

achieve any lasting success without some form of preparation.

As previously mentioned, the black American society is divided into three components as follows: the rich, the middle class, and the poor. It's not surprising, then, that those at the lower level of black society are those mainly at a disadvantage. I place the emphasis on "disadvantage" rather than being "victims," as many may consider themselves. This disadvantage is brought about by the failure of government and by their own failure as well. This will become evident, as will be seen in our presentation in this chapter and in those that will follow.

Before we continue, however, it should be clear that America is responsible for the economic disparities between the rich and the poor. For example, the legacy of discrimination and bigotry plays an important part in this dynamic. And with the passage of time, this hasn't disappeared. Hopefully, this book will bring awareness to the underlying problems or serve as a reminder to those who aren't aware of the roots of the problems facing young black men in the cities and towns in this country.

It's true that education and training are some of the keys to success! Unfortunately, with a criminal record, one will not be qualified for student loans in order to attend college. More often than not, many of those with records will not be able to get well-paying jobs. These people, in many cases, are doomed to living at the poverty line and/or below it.

It's clear that a nation will not advance when a segment of its people is in poverty. The United States is an advanced and wealthy nation—or is it? Well, I will let you be the judge of that. In any case, we are lagging behind many nations in areas such as educating our people, race relations, etc. These have resulted in a paralysis that must be cured before America will be able to heal. And frankly, there is a lot of healing to do.

What is of concern to us in this book, though, is the advancement of our young black men and women. The family structure would be the appropriate place to direct the instructions. However, due to the breakdown of the family unit, especially those in many inner cities, I have decided to write not necessarily to parents and guardians but to young black men and women themselves. This doesn't necessarily mean that parents and

A Message to Black America

guardians are exempt from the book, however!

The first thing I want to stress here is the importance of an educated and trained mind. On an individual basis, no one will gain economic independence without some form of plan and investments in the future. One of the ways to go about this is through the acquisition of knowledge. Indeed, knowledge is an important key. For example, hitting the jackpot without the knowledge how to retain the wealth will be disadvantageous to the holder of the jackpot! The money will soon depart due to lack of knowledge. "The fool and his money will depart, but wisdom, knowledge, and understanding will abide."

Please note that when refer to education, we aren't referring to those who are affluent and are able to send their children to higher institutions of learning. We are not concerned about professions or professional people. The target audience here are young black men and girls who are living in the inner cities, blacks that are living at the poverty line, and those below it—blacks who, in fact, should have been through the school system, graduated from high school, and gone on to attend technical schools or community colleges. This is important, and anyone who fails to realize this is missing the boat completely.

Please note that there are many technical skills to choose from! I wound not attempt to list them all here. The fact is that selecting a skill is an individual choice. One may prefer to become an electrician, an electronics technician, an auto mechanic, etc.

Whatever skills one would like to pursue, it's clear that one must pass through the various stages of the educational process! Please note further that your country is in need of skilled craftsmen. And you owe it to yourself and your family or prospective family to prepare for the future.

Engaging in manual, unskilled tasks should be a "means to an end," as they say. In other words, one can engage in tasks like digging a ditch, pushing a broom, and things of the nature with the aim in mind to accumulate enough money to go to school and acquire a skill. This is perfectly understandable, and it is acceptable. Skilled craftsmen command reasonable salaries

A Message to Black America

in comparison to those who are permanently engaging in the manual tasks mentioned above. And so, knowledge is the way to lift oneself and one's race out of poverty. But in almost every case, unfortunately, many who are at the poverty line and below did not prepare for the future. It may not have been their fault. It may have been a lack of partial guidance. As a result, we will guide those who are misguided and in need of direction.

We will show them the ways to success if they have the will and desire to succeed. Below, we have presented the main message that will give some form of direction to those who have missed out on the important things of life! And so, the message is intended to motivate, inspire, and direct those who are lagging behind into becoming excellent American citizens!

The Message to Young Black Men and Women

The message that we are sending here is very clear, straightforward, and to the point. And since radical change is necessary, mincing words or disguising facts is out of the question. The truth as it applies to many inner-city black youths must be told. And as promised, we will bring to attention the correct paths in which they should go. We aren't condemning or disparaging those of you who found yourselves in situations in which you feel hopeless. The fact is that there is hope! From this point onward, you will be given hope, and you should strive for the expectations that are necessary to forge ahead to a brighter future. You will be in a position to strive, not merely "get by." In later chapters, we will continue to provide additional information that will be relevant to you in your desire for a brighter future.

Here are the three important words of wisdom:

1. Whatever you do, you should educate yourself as much as you can
2. You should invest positively in the future
3. Please stop considering yourself to be the victim of circumstances

We will analyze these statements to determine their relevance in the scheme of things. It should be noted, however, that most if not all of the problems facing young black men in

A Message to Black America

the inner cities can be traced to the absence of one or more of the suggestions in this message! Some of the paralysis that is afflicting the above mentioned is self-inflicted while others represent failure at the hands of the government. In any event, young black men must lift themselves up by the bootstraps and move on to gain economic prosperity.

Please, let's examine the latter in this series. Suggestion number three: stop being victims of circumstance since this, in my opinion, is a major factor behind poverty in the inner cities and towns as far as young blacks are concerned.

Stop Being Victims of Circumstances

The concept of being a "victim of circumstance" is a major factor that we will analyze first, the reason being that there is no member of the black communities in this country who is a victim of circumstances in terms of lack of opportunities.

The opportunities are there. They are there all over this nation for blacks and others. However, many have failed to grasp the opportunities because of their own failure! They aren't prepared. And this places them at a disadvantage. Why is it that so many foreign nationals are granted permission to come and work in the United States? Simply because there is a shortage of skilled Americans! This applies not only to blacks but to Americans of all racial and ethnics groups. Our concern here is related to young black men and women, in some cases. And since men are supposed to be the head of the family, the burden is on them more so than women.

Please understand that your ancestors were the victims. They were the ones who were oppressed, victimized, and forced to labor without reward. They weren't given reparations for their contributions to America. Nevertheless, blacks in the United States today, especially those whose ancestors were enslaved in America, are victors. Yes, victors. Victors in that, black people do have equal rights and justice under the prevailing laws of this country. In the not-too-distant past, this was not the case—far from it! There is no limitation as far as opportunities for black people are concerned. The only limitation there is, is the limitations that one placed on oneself. Please note that although

A Message to Black America

the educational system leaves much to be desired, blacks are able to attend school if they wish. And besides, this is free from the elementary level up to the level of high school education.

In terms of a higher education—college, university, etc.—student loans are available. If you aren't a convicted person, your chance of getting student loans is good. But there is a catch. Student loans must be repaid. I frankly believe that black students should be exempt from repayment of government student loans. This should be a form of reparation in connection with your ancestors, the ex-slaves. I am making a suggestion here; those with the "victim" mentality needs to pick themselves up and make something of themselves. If you are one of these people, I invite you to modify your ways of thinking since this is not the case, at least not since the beginning of the twentieth century.

This victim's mentality syndrome is another fallacy, synonymous with that of "crying wolf." Remember, if blacks are qualified, they will be able to be successful! They will be able to complete. There would be no need for the government to be granting working visas and work permits to foreign expatriates. Many are coming in and taking advantage of well-paying job opportunities. Please note that there are urgent needs for professionals and semi-professionals in this country. And due to a shortage of qualified Americans, the government has no choice but to grant permission to those from foreign nations to do the jobs that young blacks and others aren't qualified to do. America should be exporting skilled engineers, technicians, etc., all over the globe. Instead, we are actually inviting these people to come in and help us.

Indeed, the black society in this country needs to produce more professionals of all levels. Too many young blacks in the inner cities are lagging behind when they should stand up and be counted. And this is to the disadvantage of everyone in black American society! The fact is that these young blacks are in need of directions. And wealthy and intellectual blacks aren't doing squat—zilch, zero—about it. Am I right about this? I stand to be corrected, but as far as I know, this is the case.

A Message to Black America

The question is, what has happened to our rich and middle-class black Americans? In addition, what has happened to our black intellectuals? What has happened to the executives in the civil rights movement organizations? What plan do they have to turn the tide facing young black men in the inner cities around? I believe that they should launch the proposed organization that I have in mind: The Early Black Education and Mentoring Association. As mentioned, the proposed organization would see to it that blacks received a quality education, gained at least one marketable skill, and became upright and productive citizens in all departments. Without self-control and discipline, one will be always in trouble. And our rich and intellectual blacks should come forth and give direction to young, inner-city black men who are at the poverty line.

Many other ethnic groups have in place well-established organizations to help their people. Some even grant interest-free loans to people of their own race. Question: Why is it that our wealthy blacks cannot launch a system of banks to grant interest-free loans to members of their race who want to start up businesses across the cities and towns in this country? Think about it. Go into any gas station anywhere in America, and who will be at the counters? They are almost always foreign employees. Foreigners come in and see the opportunities, and they make use of them. Meanwhile, our people failed to see current and future opportunities.

Well, what about taxi drivers in cities and towns? When is the last time you saw a black taxi driver? You talk about foreign accents—many taxi drivers cannot even speak the English language, or at least not American English. All these jobs should be held by young black men. Instead, they are crying "victims," "victims," "victims."

For God's sake, let's teach our young black men in the cities how to be men. How can the black American society hope to come of age when the next generation is stagnant? That is, lagging behind; semi-illiterate, undisciplined, unskilled, etc.? Action is needed. And so, I call on black America to wake up. Wake up and give a helping hand to your people who are in distress.

A Message to Black America

Let's move on to the next part of the message in this process; educating of oneself is important. In fact, ignorance is a road that leads to disaster more often than not. Let's read and contemplate the importance of an educated mind.

Principle 1: Educate Yourself

The importance of educating yourself is the next item in connection with the message. Now, please be advised that education is a lifelong process! And passing through the public education system is only the beginning on the road through life. In fact, it is said that "one never stops learning," and this is a fact! One should open one's mind to learn new things at all times, and there are many things to be learned.

Indeed, learning is a lifelong process. I myself am still learning. And the older one becomes, the more one will realize that there are still many things to be learned. One of the ways in which to learn is through the news media: newspapers, television newscasts, radio newscasts, etc. Any one or all of the above are rich sources of local, national, and international information.

First and foremost, one should be informed about what's happening in local cities and towns. In addition, a very good understanding as to what is transpiring across the nation should not be ignored. Unfortunately, there are people who do not know the name of the mayor in the city in which they live. It may not be convenient for many to read the daily newspapers, but local radio and televisions newscasts will bring news to inform you about local and national developments. The world newscast is a great source of information relative to what is transpiring across the nation, not only the current situation nationally but international matters as well. You are encouraged to be informed in any way possible. This will give one a bird's eye view of things that are happening in this nation and around the world.

In addition to all of the above, it's a good idea to visit your local library. At your local library, you will find a wealth of all sorts of information! One can learn many things by reading books, and there are thousands of them at libraries. However, its takes discipline, determination, and a willingness to improved oneself to do this. Many of the younger generation of Americans are inclined

A Message to Black America

to spend their time pursuing trivial matters rather than investing in improving themselves. And so I strongly suggest that if you are one of those people, you should find time for self-improvement. It's not good for one to go through life not knowing what is going on in your country and around the world. And remember, ignorance is no excuse!

I was recently having a discussion with one of my white neighbors, and he told me point blank that "young black men are only interested in drugs and sex --." We were having a discussion in connection with recent trouble facing young, inner-city blacks in terms of crime and violence when he made the statement. He told me that his remark is not his own viewpoint but is the general opinion of many white people in general. As a black man, I was embarrassed but not disappointed by his perspective. The question is, is the statement factual? Well, you be the judge on the matter.

So, there you are. The conduct of a minority of young, inner-city black men is casting dispersion on every young black man in this country. We cannot continue to allow such disparaging comments to continue.

Remember, the comment stems from the impression that people of other races have been given by young black men. Black America should be proactive in trying to turn this sort of impression around. And this can only be achieved through an educated mind.

Education also comes from within! This means that one should take time to quiet oneself so as to listen to the inner voice. Here is how to go about his. Take a little time to be still. Be silent and listen to what is going on inside on you. That means that you should not be distracted during your quiet time. No TV, no radio, no computer, etc. And please remember that the human consists of three parts: body, mind, and soul (spirit). Your religious leaders can give you confirmation in connection with this fact. Whatever you do, you should understand that this soul has all the answers to your problems. Therefore, please get yourself acquainted with your inner self and begin to bring about the necessary changes in your life situation!

Yes, education is the key—the master key to all success and

A Message to Black America

happiness. Therefore, please go for it by any means necessity.

And now, let's move on to instruction number two: invest positively for the future. There is a very good reason for saving this second instruction in this series for last. This will be apparent, as you will understand as we present the facts to you in a moment.

Invest Positively for the Future

A positive investment in the future is something that everyone is working to accomplish—or *should* be working to accomplish. Investing positively in the future is the purpose behind an education. This is the very reason that parents and guardians send a child to school in the first place. However, the responsibility of parents and guardians legally ends at the age of between eighteen and twenty-one, depending on the state in which you live. And if the child hasn't been exposed to the educational process between the legal age mentioned, then the child will be at a disadvantage. The young adult, therefore, is responsible for himself or herself from then on. This is not to say that parents do not have a moral responsibility to the child after the child has reached the legal age of adulthood. However, from a legal perspective, their responsibility is terminated! And the child, in all probability, must carve out his own future and destiny.

If the young adult happens to have been educated before he leaves this parents' home, he is probably equipped with a marketable skill, a profession, or some other meaningful ways to earn a livelihood. And so, the young adult should be able to provide for himself and his connections. He may fall in love, if he hasn't already, and will probably get married. And if he is wise, he will make positive contributions toward the future. Now, this future is the thing we will be discussing as we continue.

Suppose the child in our discussion weren't exposed to an education, for whatever reason, while under the care and supervision of the parents or guardians. What would be the future of that child? The child is probably illiterate and is in need of educational assistance. In fact, there are many adults who have found themselves in such positions. And so, we have a program specifically designed for people who are in this situation!

Pease note that every adult has approximate forty-five

A Message to Black America

working years to work and take care of his family and himself while preparing for the future before retirement. After retirement, between the age of sixty-five and seventy, it is said to be downhill from then. As a result, time is relatively short in terms of the allotted years given to man. Note further that "the years of our life is three score years and ten." But by reason of good health and strength, it's possible to outlive the appointed time. Note further that a score is twenty. Thus, three score (three times twenty) plus ten gives us a grand total of seventy years. This is the allotted time of man! Past the age of seventy, one is said to be "living on borrowed time." And yes, there are people who live to be ninety and over!

It goes without saying, then, that one must prepare for the future. And this should be clear in your mind from now on. There are too many blacks who end up on the streets when they reach the ripe old age of retirement. In fact, many have ended up on the street well before the age of seventy, and this is unfortunate! This is the reason that I cannot overstress the importance of preparation. It's clear that there are too many young black men wasting precious times on trivial pursuits instead of trying to make a decent living for themselves and their connections.

There are troublemakers in many black communities. And this is the result of poverty, which is the mother of ignorance. These troublemakers who are bringing disgrace on black communities and on themselves should turn from their ways and be upright citizens. In fact, the statistics on crime and violence as it relates to young black men are cause for concern. Why do they believe that harming one another with pistols and committing robbery will be the answer to their problems? This is a deadly game. And many end up behind bars while others lose their lives. The prisons, unfortunately, are full of these wrongdoers all over this nation, and there is no end in sight. We will address this issue and make relevant suggestions for the cure as we continue in the chapters.

Please, please, understand: It's wrong to take things that don't belong to you. It should never be forgotten that stealing does have its punishment. In many countries, for example, the penalty for stealing is dismemberment or even death. In this country, however, this is not the case. In any event, many people have lost their lives by breaking in and stealing.

A Message to Black America

"Thou Shall Not Steal" and "Thou Shall Not Kill" are two of the Ten Commandments! And whether or not one is caught by the authorities, it makes no difference in terms of punishment. The all-seeing eyes of Providence see everything, and one will pay sooner or later. Please note that the wrath of God will come upon those who steal, kill, etc. The fact is that punishments are often twofold: the punishment of man and the punishment of an offended Providence. It should be further noted that ignorance of Providential laws is no excuses.

You were given a mind and brain to be of service to yourself and others. As such, honesty is the best policy! And remember, no one can hide from the all-seeing eyes of the Creator of the Universe. One may evade the laws of man, but no one will evade the all-seeing eyes of an offended God. Therefore, to those who are bent on committing crime and violence, I say to them: Please stop and turn yourself around. Do not continue to bring destruction upon yourself, your race, and your family. It may be tempting for someone to take something that doesn't belong to them. This is, in most cases, is due to poverty. But think of the shame and disgrace that often follows. Think of being arrested and thrown in jail. Think of the money that will be required for posting your bail. This makes no sense to me, but it's true that poverty will drive some people to do desperate things. One should think of the consequence beforehand.

And so, I have presented the main points to you in this chapter! Other messages of importance will be given in the chapters that follow!

Please note that in past chapter, we have briefly discussed five principles for success. And I promised that I would go into them in detail in terms of analyzing them for further clarification. Therefore, let's continue the process to determine their relevance in the scheme of things.

Definitions of the Five Principles

In chapter two, we have presented five principles for success. These principles are important in the life of every young black man and woman. I invite you to pay attention to them and bring them to the attention of every young black boy and girl. The following,

A Message to Black America

therefore, are the definitions of the five principles.

A formal education is essential for success. This means that one should go to school. A child should not quit school until graduation. Dropping out of school for whatever reason will have negative consequences on the individual throughout his entire life! The objectives should be to complete the elementary school process, go on to high school, and not drop out. After the completion of high school, one should go on to learn at least one marketable skill. To acquire marketable skills, one should attend a community college or a technical school. There are many such institutions to choose from, the choices are limitless.

Those who possessed the necessary aptitude requirements may continue on to an institution of higher learning. Please note that there are many ways to acquired success, and educating oneself is a good way to recognize success when it presents itself. As a result of the fact, **Principle One: Educate Yourself** is indispensable. Therefore, whatever your calling is in life, you must recognize that education is indeed the master key.

If remedial action is necessary in terms of continued education, you have a duty and responsibility to pursue this in your own interest and in the interest of your future connections. In fact, if you happen to be lagging in areas that you believe are in needs of improvement, I strongly suggest that you seek remedial action.

Principle Two: Don't Run Afoul of the Law

As you probably are aware, young black men are disproportionately often involved in criminal activity—either at the receiving end of a crime or as the perpetrator. This plays into the problems of black-on-black crimes, especially for young blacks at the poverty line in the inner cities and towns across the nation. In addition, they make up a disproportionate segment of the inmates in penal institutions. And the reason behind this is clear: It's directly or indirectly linked to poverty and ignorance! And so, this trend, running afoul of the law, is a problem facing young black men. The way to go about reversing and preventing this trend, again, is through the process of education and training.

The first steps in the process, therefore, begin in the home. Kids who demonstrate the propensities for violence should be counseled very early. For example, they should not have the tendencies of hitting other children. They should be taught that instead of taking matters into their own hands, they should appeal to authority: parents, guardians, teachers, etc. In the school setting, this is even more serious. If a child happens to get hit by another child, he should not hit back. Instead, the child should inform the teacher. This "hitting back" dynamic often results in all sorts of problems, including but not limited to lawsuits. Parenting is a serious business, and the task is not for irresponsible people.

I often overhear parents telling their children, especially boys, that they should not be weak and that they should not let other kids pushed them around—that they should learn to defend themselves, etc. Frankly, I totally disagree with this notion. This is setting the stage for confrontation later in life.

You should be aware of the fact that the authorities are there to resolve conflicts, dispense justice, and administer punishment. If someone wants to get into a fight with you in the workplace, for example, your duty is to report it to your supervisors. Not to confront the person and take matters into your own hands. This is also true in public and other private places. In the case that you are accosted anywhere, you should bring it to the attention of law enforcement personnel. Many confrontations often turn deadly. At all cost, try and avoid confrontation with others. "One who runs from a fight will live to run from another fight."

Now, here are some suggestions in connection with staying out of trouble. It's very easy to get into trouble, but one should make sure that one is on the right side of the law. Therefore, "you should not steal, you should not kill," and you should not involve in any forms of unlawful activities. Above all, one should obey the instruction of police. Please understand that the police are empowered with authoritative license. The power to take one into custody and also the power to injure or even take a life! As a result, you should not confront the police; this is a bad mistake. If one is confronted by the police, one shouldn't resist. Instead, one's full cooperation should be given to the police. And whatever you do, please do not point a weapon at the police!

I often overhear conversations about young blacks and the police. Many people are of the opinion that young black men are dumb to confront the police. In the first place, an honest and upright citizen will do whatever is necessary to stay out of trouble. One should try to be upstanding and live an upright life that is beyond reproach. And so I invite my reader and everyone to be upright and to stay out of trouble. And whatever one does, please not run afoul of the law.

Principle Three: Stay Away from Mind-Altering Substances

Staying away from all forms of mind-altering substance abuse is the third principle in the series. Everyone will admit that a sober and focused mind is a productive mind as opposed to a mind that is strung out on narcotics. No one should subject themselves to altering the mind with illegal narcotics. It has been proven time and time again that people who find themselves in an addictive habit often end up in a negative state of mind, body, and soul. And as far as our children at the school-age level are concerned, this is an unfortunate situation. These young adults have no business experimenting with mind-altering substances. In fact, this narcotics problem is not limited to young, black city-dwellers alone. This is a gigantic problem right across the spectrum!

There are many adults who are responsible for introducing marijuana and other illegal substances to our children, and this is rather unfortunate. The fact is that drugs are paralyzing our people, and this is not acceptable. Frankly, I believe that the people who are responsible for selling illegal narcotics in back communities should be put away for life. For one thing, they aren't friends of black people in the first place. Secondly, they are the ones who are holding down young black men and women by paralyzing then with illegal narcotics. These people are enemies of black people whether they are black, white, or brown. And worse, if they are black, this goes to show how ignorant they truly are! They are crippling their race and not knowing it.

What we are concerned with here is awareness of the lagging behind of many young black men in the inner cities and towns in America due to narcotic substance abuse and other paralysis. Therefore, my advice is that these people should stay away from all forms of mind-altering substances. People who are high on the drugs often run afoul of the law, and this is to their disadvantage!

A Message to Black America

It is a known fact that many people with low morale often find it difficult to face the real world without getting high. As a result, many turn to the use and abuse of illegal substances. In fact, drugs are the blinder that many are wearing to avoid facing the facts of life. But this is not the right and proper way! Facing life without the blinder is the better way. In that case, one will be able to see things as they are in a clear and unaltered manner. There is no reason to be dependent on things external when one has the power within! This power is the one we are all born with, given to solve all of our problems. And so we should be able to get in touch with the power in order to resolve our daily problems.

I have witnessed many adults who were doing well and, for reasons unknown, started engaging in the use and abuse of illegal substances. Many of these people spiraled down to a point of no return. Manny of them lost their jobs, their homes, and their families. Eventually, they became homeless. I admonish you, please stay away from becoming a victim as so many others have become. And, frankly, black American society can do without these people who are bringing disgrace on every member of the community.

It would appear as if this drug culture habit is very hard to break. "Once hooked, always hooked," as they say. Those who aren't involved in doing drugs, I lift my hat to them! May they flourish and prosper in all their earthly undertakings.

And so I say to you, be upright in all your undertakings. Maintain strict discipline and respect yourself. Last but not least, engage in noble and meaningful activities that will bring credit to yourself, your family, and your race. And remember, the Lord helps those who help themselves!

Principle Four: Do Not Get Pregnant While in School

The fourth principle in this series is related to pregnancy in school-age girls. And this applies not only to the parents but also to the future of those involved. Early childhood pregnancy at the lower socioeconomic level is a problem with inner-city girls, and this has hit hard, especially in black communities. Frankly, something should be done about this.

You are probably asking, "What can be done about this?" Well, this entails education, education, and more education. And

A Message to Black America

this is the responsibility of parents or guardians. Dropping out of school due to pregnancy is a losing situation. And as a result, this principle is designed and written to discourage early pregnancy and to motivate girls and boys at the school-age level to abstain from sexual relationships until they are ready to take on the responsibilities of parenthood. This isn't as difficult as it seems. And so, abstinence will eventually pay its price in gold.

Abstinence from promiscuity and sexual encounters should be observed, especially when it comes to children and young adults who aren't ready to become parents. The questions of illicit sexual activities in the inner-city black communities are cause for concerns. And, frankly, as a group of people, we should prevent this ongoing problem from continuing to desecrate black American communities and their people.

Poverty begets poverty, as they say! And so we must raise the bar for our children, our race, and ourselves. How can we hope to be expecting when we have nothing for ourselves, our women, and our culture? It's time that our young men and women cease and desist from letting their hormones get the better of them. As mentioned, poverty begot poverty, and this will be the curse on our young men and women caught in the cycle of taking on responsibilities they aren't ready to handle. The problem of the child support phenomenon is a serious one. The court system is merciless with fathers who refuse to support their children.

This article is written for young girls at the school-age level since they are the ones who often suffer the consequences of early pregnancy. Indeed, young boys and young men aren't exempt. They will and often do suffer the consequences of getting girls pregnant when they aren't ready to take on the responsibilities of fatherhood. In any event, early childhood pregnancy is problematic not only for young girls and boys but also for parents and guardians. Due to biological factors, young girls often bear the brunt of this problem. They are the ones that will drop out of school. And, unfortunately, once out of school, the probability of returning is almost always zero. There are exceptions to the rule; however, all things being equal, this is often the case unless the parents are financially able to step in and render the necessary financial assistance.

Now, you can understand the consequences behind this.

A Message to Black America

Let's paint the picture more clearly: the child became pregnant at, let's say, the age of thirteen, fifteen, or sixteen years of age. At some point during the pregnancy, she will drop out of school. After the birth, she must stay home for a period of time. And so, the time that is missed between those periods of time is lost in terms of acquiring her education. Nevertheless, if the girl is lucky enough to have parents who will see to it that the child returns to school, this would be to her advantage. However, in almost if not all instances, this is not the case. As such, this girl will need to fend for herself and her child. Well, you get the picture, don't you? Remember, this girl did not receive a formal education. She has no skill to earn a livelihood. And so, she is at a disadvantage.

This is not a fictional scenario. This happens in real-life situations. And this is a blemish on black communities across the nation.

Therefore, my advice is that young girls stay in school and get an education. Also, they should stay away from sexual relationships until they have finished school and are ready to become responsible mothers. This is the message that parents should pass on to their girls and boys. If this were the case, the black communities would be prosperous! There would not be an overwhelming abundance of poverty amongst inner-city blacks. We can do much better, and we should start doing better.

Indeed, poverty begets poverty! This is evidenced in government social programs. I sincerely hope and pray that our young black men and women will stop lagging behind and will begin to be productive citizens. I know that this is possible. And it's only a matter of time before our people gain economic parity with their white counterparts.

We can do better, and we are going do better.

When people have skills, they have choices. The fact is that a man should have at least one skill! Let's contemplate the last of the five principles for success

Principle Five: You Should Acquire Marketable Skills

The final episode in this series is the fact that young adults should acquire at least one marketable skill. The reason behind

A Message to Black America

the fact should be obvious to everyone. This is particularly true in the case of young, inner-city black men. Here is the order in which things should be bone:

1. The child should attend school from elementary to high school without dropping out. After graduating from high school, the young adult should go to a technical high school or community college so as to acquire at least one skill or trade.

2. After graduation, the young adult should get a job or launch a business so as to provide for himself and his prospective family.

3. He or she probably will fall in love. Well, you know the story. "Love and marriage go together like a horse and carriage; you can't have one without the other."

This is where most of the critical aspects of life come into the equation! Nevertheless, assuming that the young adult "tied the knot," in most cases, children will be in the picture.

Please note the order in which things should transpire in the lives of a child all the way into young adulthood. And, yes, there are exceptions to the rule. However, there may have been some variations of the process. The important thing here is that the individual gets an education and acquires a marketable skill. The point being stressed is that a person with a skill will be able to make a decent living. This is not to say that one will not be able to make a livelihood without a skill. Nevertheless, skilled people have the advantage over and above unskilled laborers.

Before we conclude this chapter, I would like to make it clear that the duty and responsibilities of a man, in terms of a family structure, is more than providing food, clothes, and shelter. He has a duty to bring up his child, or children, in the right and proper manner. Suppose, for example, he himself was not brought up in the proper manner. How will he be able to bring up this next of kin in the proper manner? This may be virtually impossible. And this is, more often than not, the sort of problem facing many inner-city blacks at the lower economic end of the ladder. The time has come for turning things around for the better.

Again, where are the wealthy blacks, the intellectuals and

those who are fighting for the rights of blacks through civil rights organizations? Okay, they aren't involved.

And so I am calling on blacks to pool their resources and launch an organization so as to help their young blacks to move forward to prevent them from lagging behind.

Before we bring this chapter to its conclusion, here is a word of wisdom. "The years of our life are three score years and ten, so help us O' Lord to number our days so that we may apply our self unto wisdom."

In this chapter, we have presented major information that is of paramount importance.

It will not be necessary to go over them in their entirety. However, here are some main points that should be taken into consideration. Educating oneself is a wise and prudent investment. This is followed by an investment in the future. Man has approximately forty-five working years to work and support himself and his connections while preparing for retirement. This is based on the "three score years and ten" principle. In addition, you were taught that blacks aren't victims of circumstances as many young, inner-city blacks may believe. In fact, they are more than conquerors—victors, if you will! Yes, the opportunities are there. Go and qualify yourselves and take advantage of them.

Additionally, five principles for success were presented. To reacquaint yourself with those principles, you are encouraged to reread this chapter. In a nutshell, *A Message to Black America* is intended to motivate young black men who are lagging behind into taking their future into their hands and propelling themselves to excellence.

Many young, inner-city black men don't receive the support and guidance that they should. And this is almost always the root of the problem. We will continue to discuss this matter in the next chapter.

Chapter Four
Many Young Black Men Receive No Support

Black America should put in place a system so as to monitor, motivate, and mentor their less fortunate people. And this is especially true for many young, inner-city black men.

The reason has been that they are supposed to be the head of the family. And if this is not the case, then, there will always be problems in terms of failing family structures. In fact, this is the root of the problems as far as the breakdown in the family structure is concerned. The truth is, young black men aren't receiving the support that they so desperately needed, and this lacking of support has a devastating effect on black families at the lower level of the socioeconomic spectrum.

However, there are always exceptions to any rule, and there is an exception to this. There are inner-city black families who have enjoyed or are enjoying stable homes and family lives. They have brought up or are bringing up children to be responsible men and women—productive citizens, I may say! And many of them are doing well, to the credit of themselves, their parents, and their race! Nevertheless, this is not the case with the overwhelming majority of people in the inner cities. And they are the people we are referring to in this book.

Young black men who weren't fortunate enough to fall into

Many Young Black Men Receive No Support

the category mentioned above are at a disadvantage—those who simply didn't receive the necessary support that they needed to function as the head of the family or to pass on to their next of kin the necessary values that they need to function satisfactorily in society. And so, the root of this problem can be traced back centuries in the distant past. We will get to the bottom of this to determine who these culprits truly are, those who have set the stage for the failure of young black men.

Before we continue, please let me once again remind you of the fact that modern blacks aren't victims of circumstances as many of them in the inner cities often believe. After Reconstruction, all these things have changed! Young blacks are able to forge ahead and make something of themselves.

Indeed, they are victors in the truest sense of the word. And why is this, you may ask? Well, it is a fact that they, blacks, have managed somehow to triumph over all adversity. It is not necessary to go into specifics to point out the many and varied past adversities. However, just to remind you of some of the unfortunate things that took place in the past, we can site the question of the segregated drinking fountains and the restriction from certain restaurants, hotels, and even public schools. God willing, those days are over and gone forever!

And now, young, inner-city black men and women have the opportunities to make good, to do something uplifting, and they failed miserably. This is regrettable. Many of these fellows failed to see the light, the opportunities that are before them. And so, we will provide the necessary motivational encouragement in order to turn around young, inner-city blacks who are lagging behind. We will walk them through the steps that they should take so as to be productive citizens. You are already aware of the importance of an educated mind and, in addition, a skill, vocation, etc. As a result, let's move on to present additional information that is of major importance.

Young Blacks Received No Support

The failure of young, inner-city black men is not a recent occurrence. And this is the inherent legacy of the past! Their ancestors simply have passed down the malfunctioned program

Many Young Black Men Receive No Support

they received, which is still in place today. Remember, historically, they weren't allowed to be educated. And as for having marketable skills or vocations, that was out of the question. And who is the culprit behind this? I leave this for you to find out.

We often overhear the proverb "Give a man a fish and he will eat the fish; teach a man how to fish, and he will fish when he wants to eat fish." That is, he will fish for life. There is a moral to this story. It simply means that it's far better to give a person a skill so that they will be able to help themselves rather than to keep helping them at all times—giving these handouts if you will, in a nutshell, leads to dependence rather independence.

This dependency dynamic has passed down from generation to generation. Instead of instilling in these people a program of education and training so that they will be able to provide for their families and themselves, they were taught to wait for handouts. These people were shortchanged. And this legacy is still alive today!

In terms of housing, the new freemen were hurled into government housing projects, and this was the second mistake. Then they were given welfare and other social services on a monthly basis. Has this changed to date? No. This has not changed to date. Instead, this practice has multiplied many times over. This dependency has paralyzed many Americans, not only blacks at the lower socioeconomic level but also whites and others.

In the case of young black men, instead of seeing to it that the ancestor of the slave be educated, gain skills, and be gainfully employed, many are left in the same condition their ancestors were in many centuries ago. And since the authorities failed to come to the assistance of these people, they must fend for themselves by whatever means necessary.

You talk about theft, the sale of illegal drugs of one form or another—if you visit any housing projects, this will be evident.

There are many blacks that have made it out of the trap. And this is to their credit! Now that they are out, I believe that they have an obligation to those who are left behind. Well, where are the wealthy blacks, and why aren't they coming to the rescue of their

Many Young Black Men Receive No Support

less fortunate people? Are they not ashamed of the condition of their fellow men? They should remember that it is not necessarily about self so much as it is about the group, the race in general. "Help" should be the keyword.

Yes, there are many inner-city blacks who are receiving government assistances. These are the legacies that have been passed down from generation to generation. And I am determined to have this change. How are you going to do this? By motivating young, inner-city blacks who are lagging behind into excellence. The reason why many of these people are in the situations they find themselves in is because they know no better. Those who know better will do better. Those are the people who have made it out of the inner-city environment!

It's interesting to note that there are people in this country who strongly oppose government social programs in terms of our indigents receiving government assistance. These people oppose the American poor and indigent who are receiving government assistance. Really, who deserves government assistance? Is it *our* less fortunate or the less fortunate in some foreign country? The very thought is disgusting.

The United States government is giving aid and assistance to many foreign governments and people around the world. And those who oppose the Americans poor receiving so-called "handouts" aren't complaining about this.

Let's take a few countries into consideration. Afghanistan, for example. The United States Government gave and is still giving hundreds of billions of US taxpayer dollars to the government of Afghanistan and the people of that country. Other countries that are receiving US aid on a regular basis include but aren't limited to Pakistan, Iraq, and Israel. I firmly believe that there are enough oil-rich nations in the Middle East that should be helping their Arab brothers. It should be noted that oil-rich nations in the Middle East are very rich nations. And don't you believe that they should be assisting their Muslim brothers' nations? I firmly believe that this should be the case!

The nation of Israel, on the other hand, is receiving hundreds of billions of American taxpayer dollars, yet no one is complaining about this. However, the chump change that those on government

Many Young Black Men Receive No Support

social programs are receiving seems to conjure up jealousy and envy among many Americans. Why is this? I leave this to your imagination.

I believe that there are enough wealthy people of Israeli descent in North America and in Europe who can take care of Israel's financial matters. Just think of it—the government and the people of the nations the United States is helping are able to run circles around many Americans in terms of education. Meanwhile, there are many young black men and others in our cities who are functionally illiterate. Do you not believe that we owe it to them to educate them so that the United States can continue to remain a first-rate nation, a superpower nation? I believe so. We are far behind in math and science, etc. And we'd better catch up before it's too late or we will be the laughing stock of the world.

Oh, there are also inner-city whites and Hispanics who are at the lower ends of the socioeconomic level as well. And they need to be lifted up too. Many are the recipients of government social programs. And so, we should take care of our own before we attempt to help the governments and people of foreign nations!

In terms of the failures of many young, inner-city black men, the major reasons behind this were brought to your attention. This is an inherit situation that has affected many generations. Have you ever visited a housing project? If you have, you will quickly realize that many of them are the breeding grounds for failure. And yes, many people have made it out and have been able to make something of themselves! Those who have chosen to remain and not pick themselves up are completely lagging behind. They are doomed to failure unless they can summon the will to pick themselves up and make something of themselves.

In connection with housing projects, when you talk about drugs, robberies, rape, and murder—it would appear as if these housing projects are the birthplace of these things. And so, there are many to be blamed in this regard. Suppose, for instance, these young men who are living in these terrible situations were educated, given skills, and were gainfully employed. It is doubtful that this nation would be facing the inner-city problems it faces today, such as the slaughtering of young, inner-city black men by the police and others. As a result, I intend to present attritional

Many Young Black Men Receive No Support

information that will be useful not just to young, inner-city black men but to everyone alive and are breathing.

Before we continue further. It should be noted that there are three standards people may set for themselves and their next of kin. The standard that is set will be passed down to the next generation. If you set a high standard, your children will adapt to that standard. On the contrary, if you set a low standard, this will be passed down as well.

Below, we have presented these three standards or modes of living to contemplate. As will be seen, they aren't predicated on an affluent lifestyle. People of modest means can live a life above average, as well as those at the upper level of society!

Three Qualities of Life to Choose

In any civilized society, there are three modes of living that one can choose from. These modes aren't predicated on wealth or poverty. They are predicated on natural abilities, abilities that everyone was born with. In effect, they are God-given qualities that you will understand in a moment. But before we continue, let it be known here and now that **quality parents do raise quality children and not the other way around.**

Again, raising quality children doesn't necessarily mean that parents raising quality children should be in the upper or even the middle-class bracket. This simply means that the parents are willing to make use of the "**good principles that are within.**"

And what are those God-given qualities, you may ask?

They are the ability to control oneself: self-discipline, self-control, willpower to control the mind and the body—mind over matter, if you will. Without the realization and the control of these God-given abilities, one will make little or no progress. We will come back to these principles later in this presentation.

Indeed, it is a fact that there are parents who have found themselves in the lower economic level of societies but still raised children who turned out to be men and women of outstanding qualities. And so, poverty is not a factor in raising children to be upstanding citizens. If this were the case, then what a world this would be!

Many Young Black Men Receive No Support

And so, here are the three modes of living, as follows.

1. Average ways of life
2. Above-average ways of life
3. Below-average ways of life

Question: What mode of living do you think would produce a good way of life? Well, I leave this for you to figure out. In any event, a below-standard way of living will get one nowhere! And in fact, children living in this mode will probably pass this on to their next of kin. And the cycle continues. I do hope that you understand the dynamics of what we are talking about here. This is no fairytale; these are real facts of life and real situations. And one must choose which of these modes are relevant.

Now, let's consider the question of self-discipline, self-control, and willpower.

If one cannot discipline oneself, then all will be lost. A man must be able to discipline himself! This entails looking good, feeling good, and talking good, but it goes even further than that. This brings us to self- control: controlling the temper, for example. In a heated conversation, without controlling the temper, this can and often does result in all sorts of trouble. Later regrets are of no consequence after the trouble has occurred; it's too late.

It is said that "the devil tempts, but he doesn't force." And indeed, no one can force anyone to do something that one doesn't want to do. This is the department of the will—willpower—and it's there for you, free.

Since we are on this subject, I may as well tell you the truth. There will be always two trains of thought entering the mind. One is from Divine Providence, and the other is from the source of darkness—evil influence. You see, good and evil always coexist! As a result, good and evil thoughts are always entering the mind. Carrying out the suggestions of the wrong influence will always lead to destruction. One of the ways people often carry out evil schemes is by listening to the wrong suggestion, brought about through mind-altering substance abused. Let's take an example into consideration. Suppose someone is high on pot or any another form of drugs, for that matter. Then a silent thought enters the mind to go rob a bank, a store, or a house. Where do you think that thought originated from? Certainly this is not from the source of good: God. **The only thing that can prevent one from yielding to the robbery temptation is the will—self-control and discipline.**

Other important virtues that should be taken into consideration are patience and tolerance. There are too many impatient people who function as if there will be no tomorrow. They want everything now, now! They are intolerant and do not want to wait under any circumstances. It is said that "Rome was not built in a day." No, it took time to build Rome. One must learn to exercise patience. This world was made in seven days, according to the Scriptures. And so, patience is a virtue. Patience and tolerance go together. You may be asking, what is this tolerance? Tolerance is the capacity to endure without breaking or at least without showing signs of breaking. Sitting for an hour or two at the doctor's office, for example, without complaining, whining, or lashing out—even when hot under the collar—without anyone suspecting is a demonstration of tolerance.

These things should be taught at an early age so as to keep children and young adults in line. In fact, there are parents who have taught these things to their children. And these things can be detected in people's actions from an early age through to adulthood.

Unfortunately, there are people who cannot endure any kind of hardships without breaking down in one form or another. And this is a sign of impatience and lack of tolerance. This is not satisfactory under any circumstances. It is a prescription for disaster. In fact, these kinds of people quite often find themselves in trouble, not only with the police but also with everyone else. As a result, I am bringing to the attention of my reader the necessary steps to be taken when dealing with the police.

What to Do When Confronted by the Police

The police are supposed to be protectors of citizens and noncitizens alike. But they are human, and even though they are supposed to be functioning at a higher level, they have their likes and dislikes just like anyone else. They often make mistakes

Many Young Black Men Receive No Support

and, in many cases, at the expense of the lives of others. And so, caution is necessary when dealing with the police. You should take note that the police are given the authority to investigate crime and violence. As a result, they have the authority to arrest anyone who broke the law! It should be further noted that the police can stop, search, and arrest anyone who they suspect of wrongdoing. And so, cooperating with them is the right thing to do. Many of our people, young black men, often fail to cooperate with law enforcement personnel and, as a result, find themselves deeper in trouble. Many have even lost their lives in conflict with them. "Caution," then, is the keyword here.

Therefore, whenever one is stopped by the police, there are things that one should know so as not to bring unnecessary trouble on oneself. Below is a list of things that are necessary to do if you happen to be accosted at any time by law enforcement personnel.

But first, it's a good practice to live your life above reproach. In that case, if and when one is stopped by the police, it will not be necessary to have any fear. No need to be running away from them. We should try and be upright in all departments. Crime and violence just don't pay! If a person commits a crime, he will, in all probability, be caught sooner or later! And with current technologies, he will be caught sooner rather than later.

What is the success rate for a criminal be apprehended and brought to justice, on the scale of one to ten? What number would you estimate? Well, the success rate in this regards is very high. And so, honesty is the best policy. Dishonesty, on the other hand, is the mother of all evil. "Thou Shall Not Steal, Thou Shall Not Kill." These are laws given to man from the Almighty Creator. And violating any one of them will, in time, certainly bring Divine consequences on the transgressor!

Now, if you are approached by the police, the first thing to do is listen carefully to what they say. Secondly, you should comply and do not try to resist. If he or she says to raise your hands, you should raise your hands. You should be cooperative in all aspects of the instructions given you. Do not run; do not ever make the slightest mistake and point a weapon at the police if you want to stay alive. Do not tackle the police. Remember, he or she has the

Many Young Black Men Receive No Support

authority to maim you or even take your life.

And remember, whether you like them or not makes no difference. They are doing their jobs. You should communicate with the police as you would with your neighbors or anyone else. There are good and bad people, and the police aren't excluded. And if the police overstep, they will be in trouble just as anyone else! Again, with modern technologies, the police are often under constant scrutiny.

In recent months, I have been hearing a lot about suspects who have been accosted by the police. Quite frequently, the suspects had gotten into struggles with them, and many were even reaching for the police's weapons. Frankly, I do not know what to make of this—if this is factual in the first place. In case, you are driving and are stopped by one of them, the same instructions should be adhered to. Just follow instructions.

Recently, a motorist was shot by the police while he was in the act of getting his driver's license for them. When he was questioned by the authorities, the police officer argued that "he was in fear for his life," believing that the driver was reaching for his weapon. Unfortunately, the driver did not survive. This is not an isolated incident! These sorts of police killings and excuses happen all too frequently. The fact is that the police, like anyone else, will answer to a Higher Authority! There are many ways to disable an individual without taking his life. The truth is, those who live by the sword often die by the sword.

"Thou Shall Not Kill" And What Providence Has in Store for Those Who Do

Before we go any further, please allow me to bring to your attention some of the facts of life as they relate to things Spiritual and Divine. It should be understood that no man can commit evil and not pay the consequences! This includes but is not limited to stealing, raping, murdering, etc. He who has committed a crime against his brothers may or may not be caught by man. Nevertheless, its makes no difference. He will pay today or he will tomorrow, but paying for his evil deeds is as assured as the sun rising in the east. Taking a life, innocent or guilty, is something

Many Young Black Men Receive No Support

that "no wise man" will ever do or should ever do. Blood on one's hands is something that must be avoided at all costs, especially the blood of an innocent man.

Please note that the blood of the departed will cry out to God, and the vengeance of God will certainly descend on the guilty. It is clearly written, "vengeance belongs to me, and I will repay." People who have shed innocent blood often cannot live with themselves. And the remorse, the guilt, often reaches the point that those involved will commit suicide. This happens quite frequently. And at other times, they themselves are met with a similar fate. That is, another takes their life as well.

The question is, why it is that many people aren't aware of the truth? This nation is said to be founded on Christian principles, yet many people fail to understand the facts of life as they relate to laws, Natural and Divine. Natural and Divine Laws are silent, but they are effective. As a result, rewards and punishments are being dispensed constantly! I believe that the church has an obligation to bring these truths to light—the truth as it relates to rewards and punishment. Any and all forms of injustice committed by man will in time be addressed by Providence! This may or may not take place in this life but certainly will in the next one.

Remember, the cycle of life is relatively short—three score years and ten—seventy years. However, many people live to be eighty, ninety, or even one hundred years of age due to good health and strength.

Man came into this world helpless. And when man serves his time, he will return to his Maker. Many people have no idea as to what goes on with the soul when the soul of man departs the body and returns to where it came from in the first place, although it is written "the soul return to its maker," and "after death comes the Judgment." The truth is that "the half of the Mysteries has never been told to everyone!" There are chosen people, however, who are entrusted with secret teachings, and they are aware of many things Spiritual and Divine. What about the secret teachings of Patriarchs such as Moses and others? Remember Solomon? He was very wise, and he has left secret teachings for those who seek wisdom and knowledge. God granted great wisdom to King Solomon. And Solomon, in return, passed down portions of his

Many Young Black Men Receive No Support

wisdom to the seekers of truth.

If you remember nothing else in these presentations, there is one thing that you should never forget, and it is the fact that "man will reap that which he has sown!"

Therefore, it is in the interest of man to be upright! Do all the good that you can to all the people you can, and leave the reward to your Almighty Maker!

Before we close this chapter, there are some things that I would like to bring to your attention, and they are in connection with behavior. For Heaven's sake, please do not let children take matters into their own hands. That is, if someone happens to hit the child, whether in school or other places, they should not hit back. This could escalate out of control. If this should happen in the school, the child should complain to the teacher and let the teacher handle the matter.

What happens if someone in the workplace assaults you? How should you handle the situation? Well, you should go to your supervisor and complain. Many confrontations often end in unpleasant situations, even dismemberment or death. In case you are confronted in public, don't fight back. Call the police. Escalating a conflict will only lead to more conflict. And as you know, conflict always leads to unpleasant situations.

There are parents who tell their children that they should not let other children push them around and that they should hit back whenever they are hit by other children; they should learn to defend themselves. Now, this is the wrong attitude. And this is often a prescription for disaster. The child will grow up believing that it's okay to take matters into his own hands rather than consulting the authorities, and this is wrong!

Therefore, in all your undertakings, please exercise good judgment. Remember, you are in possession of Divine attributes that will be able to steer you in the right direction. Above all, you should try to live a life above average. If you should happen to fail, you will only go one step below, living an average life but never a life below average.

In this chapter, we have discussed major issues of importance. As a result, I invite you to read this chapter many

Many Young Black Men Receive No Support

times so as to grasp the importance of the messages. The chapter is full of information designed and written to motivate young black people who are lagging behind to be excellent citizens, to be responsible, and to be outstanding men and women.

How much do you know about the history of other black people who are your neighbors, such as those in the Caribbean Islands, Latin America, and Europe? You should get to know these people or at least their history. Remember: Ignorance is no excuse.

And so, in the next chapter, we will present a bird's eye view of the history of black people in the Caribbean, Latin America, and Europe.

Chapter Five
Black People in the Caribbean and Latin America

How much do our black American friends know about other blacks who are living in places such as in the Caribbean Islands, Central and South America, or even Europe? "Very little," many will say, while others will proclaim that they have heard about them. There are others who will confess that they know little or nothing about those people. If the answer to any of the questions above is negative, then we have a lot of work to do.

If the reader isn't well informed or educated about other black counterparts within our own hemisphere, I will bring some degree of enlightenment on the matter to your attention. After all, black people in the regions mentioned share some common heritage with you—the black American people—common heritage in that their ancestors were also from the continent of Africa, as your ancestors were.

The ship that brought your ancestors to the North America shores also discharged its human cargo of captured slaves in the Caribbean Islands. And so, let's open up this history lesson beginning with the Island of Cuba, the reason being that Cuba is in the news quite recently in terms of embargo lifting and the cancellation of blacklisting as it relates to the sponsoring of terrorism.

Black People in the Caribbean and Latin America

Cuba

Columbus sailed to Cuba in 1492 and claimed it for the Spanish Government. At the time, the Dutch and the French often raided the island, but the British captured Havana, the capital, from Spain in 1762 during the war between the British and the French. They occupied the country until 1763 when they returned it to Spain. During the British occupation of Cuba, slaves from Africa were brought in to farm the land, thus the introduction of black people to the island.

Please note that the ethnicity of the Cuban people is of Spanish (Spaniard) and African descends. Intermingling and marriages produce a third group of people, mixed Negroes and Spaniards. Remnants of the Spaniards can be seen in Cuba, but the overwhelming number of the Cuban people is a mixture of Spaniards and Africans. And so, whenever you see a Cuban brother, you should accept him as your brother.

Haiti

Haiti was originally a French colony. It won its freedom when its black population declared themselves free from France in 1804. Columbus discovered Haiti in 1492 and made it the first European colony in the New World. The French brought African slaves to Haiti in the 1600s to work on plantations. Today, 90 percent of Haitians are Negroes. The remanding 10 percent are mixed Negroes and white—mulattos.

The French offer no economic assistance to Haiti, and because of the neglect, Haiti is the poorest country in the Western Hampshire. Many Haitians come to the United States in any manner they can in search for a better life. Over the centuries Haiti has suffered many natural disasters. Haiti is far from a developing country. The people of that nation are in need of help.

And so, whenever one comes in contact with a Haitian, one will have a better understanding of his plight. For Heaven's sake, please do not turn your back on your Haitian brother, nor sister. Instead, embrace him/her. Let them know that you are aware of their plight and that you will help in whatever ways you can.

Black People in the Caribbean and Latin America

Puerto Rico

This island was a Spanish colony also, but it was surrendered to the United States during the 1898 war with Spain. Today, the Island is receiving economic assistance and military protection from the United States. However, the government of Puerto Rico has autonomy and authority in all local affairs of the island. Puerto Ricans are US citizens and have free and unlimited access to the mainland—the United States of America!

American Indians once occupied Puerto Rica before the arrival of Columbus. However, they were driven out over a period of time. Many Puerto Ricans today are the descendants of the Indians and Spaniards. In addition, with the introduction of the slaves on the island, this produced another mixed race, as will be explained in a moment.

In the 1800s, blacks were brought to the island as slaves to work on the farms and in the gold mines. And with intermarriages and intermingling with the above-mentioned people, there is another mixture. And so, the current ethnicities of the Puerto Rican people are mixtures of Indians, Spaniards, and blacks.

One should treat the Puerto Rican people as if they are blacks. After all, the black blood is in their veins! I am aware of the fact that the Puerto Rican people receive a bad rap from the America people! And this should never be the case. Please, let's be understanding to these people and let them know that the American people do care about them. And so, the next time that you see a brother from the island of Puerto Rico, you will have a better understanding of this plight.

In addition to the regions mentioned, blacks are prevalent throughout other regions of the Caribbean and Central and South America: Brazil, Panama, Mexico, etc. There are many countries in the Caribbean area that I could cite, but the above-mentioned will serve to bring to light the existence of blacks in the Caribbean Islands and Latin America. Blacks are also in Europe: Portugal and Spain, for example. Their ancestors were brought there as slaves from Africa. However; their features and complexion are changed because they are absorbed into the cultures. We will

Black People in the Caribbean and Latin America

look at the history of blacks in Europe in another chapter.

The common thread that binds blacks within the Caribbean regions, Latin America, North America, and Europe, is stronger than that which divides them. This should be taken into consideration. Black people in the Western Hemisphere can trace their roots back to the motherland of west Africa. During the slave trading era, Portuguese seamen were taking their cargoes of slaves to Europe (Portugal and Spain) and also to the New World (the Americas), while British seamen were taking their shipment to the Caribbean Islands and Central and South America.

As a result, blacks—whether they are on the islands, North or South America, or in Europe—share a common heritage! One should understand that the black race comes in many colors. And as such, we should love all people whether we are aware of a certain ethnic background or not! I sincerely hope that the information presented will go a long way in bringing awareness to the American black people.

It is said that ignorance is no excuse. This may well be the case. However, how can one be enlightened on a particular subject when one wasn't informed about the subject in the first place? The suppression of information from a race of people, it terms of its history, is to keep the race ignorant of its history. Unfortunately, this is the case in terms of the history of blacks in the Western Hemisphere. The only alternative is the historical information that is stored in public libraries. This is the reason that educating oneself is important.

And so, whatever historical information you may need can be found at the library!

Please note that I do not forget about the Island of Jamaica. Jamaica was once a British Commonwealth Nation, and it became an independent nation from Great Brain.

Below you will see a fundamental History of Jamaica.

Jamaica

Jamaica is one of many Islands in the Caribbean. In fact, Jamaica is one of over 6,000 islands within the region. Many of these islands are so small that they are not inhabited by anyone

Black People in the Caribbean and Latin America

except birds. Bird sanctuaries can be found all over these tiny lands. In addition, fishing expeditions are often led to these islands by deep sea fishing professionals.

History reveals that Christopher Columbus discovered Jamaica in 1494. Before the arrival of Columbus, Indians were the inhabitants of Jamaica. After the arrival of Columbus, they were eventually killed or driven out due to the harsh treatment they received by the Spaniard conquerors. In addition to the Spaniards, the British also invaded Jamaica in 1655 and completed their conquest in 1660. Slaves from West Africa were brought in by the British to replace the Arawak Indians working on the farms. The English fought and conquered the Spaniards and drove them out. Great Britain, the victor, received legal possession of the island under the terms of the Treaty of Madrid. Jamaica became a legal British possession in 1670. And so, Jamaica was the possession of Great Britain for over 300 years until its independence in 1962.

Interesting, isn't it?

Due to slave trading, Jamaica reached its greatest potential in the 1700s in terms of generating wealth for the British. Sugar and the slave trading business were the chief source of wealth to the British economy during that time. In fact, the island became the leading slave trading operation in the Western Hemisphere. The slave trading market, however, gradually declined after the Revolutionary War in the United States of America, and the Brutish finally freed the slaves in 1834.

After slavery was abolished, the farming of sugar cane gradually declined, and banana farming increased. Sugar, among other products, are still produced in Jamaica today to meet the nation's needs and for export. This is also true of the production of Jamaica's rum. It is said and generally believed that Jamaica's rum is the finest in the world.

Currently, Jamaica is an independent nation within the British Commonwealth of Nations and maintains close ties with the United Kingdom. The Jamaica people elect a democratic government every five years from one of two major political parties, and the governor general, the Queen's representative, appoints the PM (prime minister) to administer the affairs of the nation and of the Jamaican people.

Black People in the Caribbean and Latin America

The Jamaican Economy

Jamaica is a developing nation with many industrial foundations and businesses. In addition, Jamaica is the largest bauxite-producing nation in the world. From the mining and processing of bauxite ore, aluminum is produced. Aluminum is a metal used in all forms of metallic fabrication. Agriculture products also account for some degree of Jamaica's exports. Natural resources in Jamaica include but are not limited to gypsum, lead, marble, salt, etc. And yes, everyone is aware of Jamaica's Tories Industry. As such, millions of visitors from around the world visit Jamaica annually to enjoy the tropical climate. It is said and generally believed that the Island of Jamaica is a Tories Mecca, and rightfully so!

The pleasant, year-round climate and constant tailwinds leave visitors to the island yearning for more and more of Jamaica! Almost everyone who has been to that nation will attest to its beauty and charm.

The question of skilled craftsmen and professionals varies in Jamaica. They vary from the lowest-level vocations to scientist technologists and engineering. Please note that the educational system in Jamaica is one of the best in the world. As a former British colony, the British legacy is fully alive and well in that country. Now, let's acquaint you with some important information about the Jamaican people.

The Jamaican People

The majority of Jamaicans are a mixed race of blacks and white ancestors.

Jamaican is a multiracial society with many different races of people: blacks mixed, black and white, whites, brown, East Indians, Chinese, and others. And so the melting pot system is alive and well on the Island. This makes the Jamaican people different and distinct from other people. As the national motto indicates, "Out of many, one people"—the Jamaican people.

During the enslavement of the African people in the west their names and tribal identities were lost. Their new names

Black People in the Caribbean and Latin America

were derived from the people who owned them. Thus, names like Hudson, Burton, Brown, Walton, and so on and so forth replace true names. This is true and applicable to American blacks as well. I hope every American black is aware of this fact.

The United Kingdom and its people owe the Jamaican people much! The government and people of the Islands of Jamaica have never demanded reparation from the British for their ancestors' enslavement. And I encourage the people to bring this to the UK's attention in order for them to reconcile the breach they committed against the black people.

Religions in Jamaica are as diverse as the people. Popular religions include but are not limited to Anglican, Baptist, Methodist, Presbyterian, Roman Catholic, and Seventh Day Adventist—even the popular Rastafari cult group, who concocted their own religion. And they worship in their owns ways and in their owns rights. And so, on Sundays, the people go off to worship in many different ways across the nation.

Opposition to Blacks from the Islands and South America

There seems to be an undercurrent of some form of resentment and opposition from some members of the black communities to blacks coming from the Caribbean Islands and South and Central America. It is not known whether or not this disdain is widespread, but all indications have shown that the problem does exist. Furthermore, it isn't clear as to the reason or reasons behind the resentment. How can one explain such phenomenon?

In any event, they are your people! And now that you are aware of the history of black people in the West, it is hoped that attitudes will change.

It should be understood that whenever a stranger comes to your country, your dwelling, or your place of business, the host is obligated to welcome the guest and make the stranger feels at home! The host synonymous with the establishment, and the guest is the newcomer, the visitor, or the stranger! Good gestures are lacking in many quarters. As a result, hostility, resentment, and discord are on the rise in all walks of life here in the United

Black People in the Caribbean and Latin America

States!

Before we continue, please let me ask you a question. Have you ever heard of one Marcus Messiah Garvey? If the answer to the question is no, then you should know that he was a Jamaican who came to the Unites States to assist the black American people in their struggle for equal rights and justice. And so I will bring to your attention the fundamental history of Marcus Garvey.

Jamaican-born Marcus Garvey came to the US to show the American black people the way in which to go about organizing themselves. Marcus Garvey came to the United States with the bold and ambitious intention to organize blacks into a viable and dynamic entity, not only incorporating blacks in the US but also those in the Caribbean Islands, South America, and Africa. He formed a movement: Universal Negro Improvement Associate (UNIA).

Marcus Garvey came to the United States with the intention to start a movement and organize blacks in the West and in Africa to create a government of their own. However, this movement was short-lived due to opposition against Garvey.

Garvey and the Pan-African Movement he founded here in the United States had far-reaching implications. To fully understand the life and works of the late Marcus Garvey, one should consult the archives of history.

In any event, Garvey sought to lift up blacks, not only those in the United States but also those in the Caribbean Islands, Central and South America, and in Africa and others areas mentioned.

Marcus Garvey was born in St. Ann's Bay, Jamaica in 1877. He was educated in Jamaica and became a printer by profession. As a master printer, Garvey worked as a foreman in a large printing industry in Kingston. However, he lost that job because of his defiance of his company's policy and his failure as a member of management when he went on strike in support of the printers he was supposed to be micromanaging.

The government of Jamaica hired Garvey shortly thereafter as a printer. He was employed as a printer at the government printing office in Kingston. He remained with the government for many years until he immigrated to the United States in 1916. In

Black People in the Caribbean and Latin America

the United States, Marcus Garvey was a dynamic and charismatic Civil Right advocate. He started his movement in Harlem. Garvey was regarded by many in the black communities as a powerful liberator. Tens of thousands gathered to listen to him whenever he gave a speech. Garvey's vision, as he declared to his followers, was to organize all blacks throughout the world into one body and establish a country and government for them.

His messages resonated with many; it brought hope and inspiration to millions of black people from all walks of lives. Garvey proclaimed that black people should form themselves into a viable entity, take control of their future, and not depend on white America but instead depend on themselves.

Garvey emphasized self-reliance, self-esteem, and self-improvement. One of Garvey's objectives for blacks in the United States and in the Caribbean Islands was education. Higher education all the way to the college level was instilled in his followers. He emphasized, among other things, the importance of technical and managerial skills for black people and that every black should acquire at least one profession—a marketable skill.

Naturally, everyone was enthused with the messenger and his messages. And so, Garvey fired up people everywhere, and everyone wanted a piece of him. This civil rights advocate was determined to organize black Americans into a positive, dynamic force. He inculcated self-discipline, self-reliance, and a positive attitude in his followers.

Regrettably, though, Garvey's vision to unify the black race didn't materialize. He was forced out of the United States, as we will see later. If Garvey's vision for the black people had come to fruition, things would have been different, not only for American blacks alone but also for black people in Africa and those throughout the world.

Garvey's Pan-African movement encourages blacks to develop themselves and Africa for all black people everywhere. One of his visions was to see the end of Europeans' domination and plundering of Africa's resources. His vision of a developed Africa for Africans and the expelling of Europeans from the continent never materialized.

Black People in the Caribbean and Latin America

People who attended Garvey's meetings liked what they heard, and many cheered him on. With the overwhelming support Garvey received from this supporter, he went on to formed a paramilitary movement. He organized a black paramilitary group and referred to himself as the commanding chief of the force. The colorful uniforms of his freedom fighters and foot soldiers and the precision of the marching band were impressionable to millions. The pageantry of the semi-military foot soldiers electrified blacks from all over the Americas, the Caribbean Islands, and on the Continent of Africa.

Tens of thousands joined up with the Garvey's movements. They were ready and willing to participate in his call for blacks to rise up and be counted, not to remain passive and beaten down by the powers that be. He also emphasized the fact that the American black people's forefathers had labored as slaves to make this nation wealthy, that they were entitled to share the wealth of the land, and that they should not be satisfied to remain as second-class citizens.

Blacks and whites alike admired Marcus Garvey. And he gained supports from many groups, although there were those who questioned his motives and his ability to deliver. He founded a group: The Universal Negro Improvement Association, UNIA.

Blacks anticipated that Garvey had the solution to the black man's problem, and they looked forward with great anticipation for the rise of the Negroes throughout the world. He requested financial support from his followers. Funds started to pour in from all over, and Garvey launched his first business: The Black Star Line Company. This was possibly due to the contributions the organization had received from blacks across the United States. It would not last long, though; the contributions from Garvey's supporters and admirers—sent by way of the US postal service—would soon take their toll.

Charges of mail fraud were brought against Marcus Garvey during the process, and this proved to be the beginning of the end for Garvey and his movement, as will be seen in a moment.

The Black Star Line Company

Garvey started the Black Line Company in 1919. Money

Black People in the Caribbean and Latin America

was coming in from people who attended his meetings. And he encouraged his supporters that they should buy stock in the company. Money started to pour in from near and far by way of the federal mail service, and the company bought its first ship. The name of the Ship to be owned by the Company was the *Yarmouth*. The company went on to acquire two other ships thereafter. These ships were intended to transport passengers to the Caribbean, South America, and Africa. The business of shipping was not profitable, and the company began to lose money.

Sustained losses were recorded, and the business was no longer viable. And so the company went into disarray due to the loss, and Garvey's critics and opponents were having the time of their lives. Their criticism became tangible when they argued as to whether or not these propositions were viable. Many believed, however, that he might have been sincere in his undertaking but shouldn't have ventured into a business that he had no knowledge of. Others believed that Garvey was conspiring to defraud them. There were still others who bitterly opposed Garvey's objectives, and they would soon turn against him. They believed that the charismatic Garvey came from the West Indies with antiquated ideas that wouldn't come to fruition.

Well, theses trains of thought are comparable to the Israelite people not wanting to leave the land of Egypt. They complained bitterly that it would be better for them to remain slaves in Egypt that to die in the unknown territory in the desert. Please note that I used this comparison believing that you are familiar with the movie *The Ten Commandments* or the book of Exodus in the Bible.

Garvey's vision for black people everywhere probably would have succeeded had it not been for his critics and his opponents. It was believed by many that the government conspired to break the back of Garvey and his United Negro Improvement Association Movement. Whatever the case may have been, Garvey was defeated, and his vision for unifying black people—and the unification of the continent of Africa, black Africa—did not materialize!

In June 1923, Marcus Garvey, President of the UNIA and the would-be president of Africa, was found guilty of mail fraud by the government of the US. He was sentenced to five years in prison.

Black People in the Caribbean and Latin America

His supporters were furious and petitioned the US president, Calvin Coolidge, who commuted his sentence. In December of 1929, Marcus Garvey was deported from the United States.

Being a convicted felon and an alien, Marcus Garvey was deported back to his country for committing a federal crime. And so his dreams of unifying blacks in the West and those in Africa unfortunately crumbled.

Back in Jamaica, Garvey's attempts to run his Harlem office were fruitless. Garvey again met with bad luck when he was sentenced to prison in Jamaica for contempt of court in Kingston. Garvey eventually moved to England where he lived out the rest of his life, probably as a defeated man.

Naturally, Marcus Garvey blamed his opponents for his downfall. If he had succeeded with his vision, black people all over would have been unified. On the other hand, if his vision and ambition to unify and develop the continent of Africa had been realized, this would have been an outstanding accomplishment indeed.

Black Africa needs unification! Those of us who are in the West, particularly of the Negro race, should consider what it would be like to see the land of our forefathers unified and developed. Unified and developed in terms of its military, air force, navy and marines. In addition, imagine what it would be like to see Africa leading the world in manufacturing, dairy farming, and agricultural products. These were the visions of the great Marcus Garvey. But these things apparently were not to be.

We have presented the history of Garvey and his visions. Now, let's continue to look at real-life situations as they relate to the problems of young black men in the cities and towns in this country. We will examine what has motivated young blacks to be so violent against their own people.

Black-on-Black Crime

The problems of brothers against brothers are not new to the human race. This has been in effect since Cain and Abel. Now, for those of you who are Biblically grounded, you may recall that Cain killed his brother Abel out of jealousy. And when he was asked, "Where is your brother?" do you remember his answer? Cain replied, "Am I my brother's keeper?"

And this has not changed since the beginning of time! In fact, this is worsening!

Every race is guilty of this crime. However, what we are concerned about here are black-on-black crimes in this country.

The problems of black-on-black crime in the inner cities pose tremendous problems for everyone, and this raises many questions. What is the reason behind this? Why have those who are engaged in criminal activities in their black neighborhoods turned on their own black people? After many years of discrimination and segregation against this race, one would believe that young blacks who are engaged in crime and violence against their own would come together in love and unity to lift the race to a higher level. Instead, many of the criminals are turning on their own people in a violent and malicious manner. And so, those who are engaged in these sorts of things should be rooted out. It's clear, however, that poverty and ignorance are the main causes of the problem. And unless there is a reversal in the situation, it is doubtful as to whether or not these things will change anytime soon.

Now, everyone or almost everyone is aware of the narcotic problems in many black communities. Narcotics are stimulants that perpetuate violence. We are also cognizant of the fact that there are people from south of the border responsible for most of the drug trafficking problems in black neighborhoods. We must get the drugs off our streets and out of our neighborhoods. Black society has lost many of its people due to the use of illegal drugs. This poison has taken over the minds of the victims and rendered them impotent. And this cannot continue indefinitely.

It should also be noted that anyone who is supplying illegal narcotics to black communities is no friend of black people! It should be further noted that destruction of an individual goes far behind self-destruction. This is destructive to the entire black race! An addict has little or no control over his or her mind. And as such, the influence of the narcotic will drive those under its influence into stealing, raping, and all manner of wrongdoing—even the destruction of others and themselves!

Black People in the Caribbean and Latin America

I know, this may be easier said than done, but the way to prevent the above and the downfall of the individual and his race is to stay away from the use of illegal drugs. Those who are involved should get it out of their neighborhoods once and for all. If our neighbors are engaged in illicit activities, members within the communities can do something about it, can't they? And remember, your future and the future of our people, the black people, is at stake here!

We aren't dumb, are we? Poisoning our people is a curse on the perpetrator. We have the ability to rise to another level. We should begin today to pick ourselves up by the bootstraps and move ahead to success. We should do things that will enhance and advance the race instead of beating ourselves down and taking our race and people down with us.

In this chapter, we have brought to your attention historical information that you probably weren't aware of. And I am hopeful that you have found Marcus Garvey and his vision to be interesting. We also brought to your attention the history of blacks in many nations in the Caribbean and Latin America. Blacks in Europe were also discussed.

There exists a need for positive mentoring of young black men in the inner cities and towns across this nation. And so, in the next chapter, we will examine this and offer assistance.

Chapter Six
The Need for Positive Mentors

There exists a need for positive mentors and role models for young black men in the inner cities and towns across this nation. And the absence of positive role models has brought tremendous danger to our most vulnerable. This is evident, considering the amount of trouble many of these people are getting themselves into on a constant basis.

Heaven knows it's distressing watching the news these days. When will the slaughtering of young black men come to an end? It's embarrassing, and frankly, I've stopped counting the killings by police and others, even among young black men themselves. I stopped counting in March of 2015. One thing is certain, and it is the fact that if this senseless killing doesn't stop, then the black race in the United States is heading for extinction.

And so, something must be done to turn the tide. I have written this book to bring relevant information to the attentions of young black men in the lower socioeconomic level of black society. Whether they will read the book is another matter. And so I am hoping that black organizations such as Jack & Gill, the NAACP, etc., will see to it that their people get the book and read it and practice the things listed therein for their own good.

Indeed, young, inner-city black men are in need of more

The Need for Positive Mentors

positive role models! Please note, however, that we are not talking about more football stars, nor basketball stars, nor even rap artists. No, no, what we are talking about here is scientists, engineers, medical professionals, etc. These are the kinds of people that young black men need as role models. These are the people that they should be looking up to. For the most part, these professional people aren't living in the cities. These are professional people of the upper and middle-class levels who are living in the suburbs.

And so, the question is, how does one get people like those mentioned to be role models for inner-city blacks? Will they visit poor communities in order to mentor these less fortunate people? I cannot answer the question. But this is where the proposed organization mentioned, the Early Black Education and Mentoring Association, would come into the equation.

In any event, this book is full of information necessary for one to pick oneself up and make something of oneself. In effect, it's a set of instructions designed and written to effectively bring about changes to the reader at all levels.

Please note that the NAACP is a fine organization that is doing a very good job under trying circumstances for the most part. Nevertheless, this would be the ideal organization for launching the proposed Early Black Education and Mentoring Association. This civil rights organization has its hands full in defending the civil rights of its people. However, I firmly believed that this organization should reach out and render more assistance to its people at the lower end at the economic level, assistance in seeing that young black men attend school and acquire a skill. I believe that an organization dedicated to instilling positive influence in young blacks should be launched by the NAACP.

Do you remember Marcus Garvey? Well, this was one of Marcus Garvey's ambitions—to see that every black person got an education and at least one skill or trade. Garvey's ambition was the uplifting of blacks through self-reliance. That is, reliance on oneself through education and training. Unfortunately, he was brought down by his enemy.

The Need for Positive Mentors

In any event, blacks cannot expect that another race of people should do the things for them that they should be doing for themselves and their people! Self-preservation and self-reliance are the keys, and this is important as far as black America is concerned. And, as mentioned in the previous chapter, this self-reliance was one of the objectives of Jamaican-born Marcus Garvey, the founder of the ill-fated United Negro Improvement Association (UNIA). Here, we see the teaching of Marcus Garvey in terms of self-reliance spelled out clearly to black people everywhere. And as such, I firmly believe that black people themselves should engage in positive mentoring to their own people.

And so, the primary responsibilities of the organization mentioned are to develop, instill, and advance young, inner-city black men until they are able to fend for themselves. This probably seems to be a gigantic task to many of you. Nevertheless, the process would ensure that black Americans rapidly rise to a higher level! The process would advance not only an individual or groups of individuals but the entire race of black American people.

Live Your Life above Reproach

Sometime in April of 2015, I was watching the news on one of the three major TV networks, CNN, and at the lower level of the screen, an interesting headline scrolled across the screen as follows: "Black men go to prison, white men get rich." It wasn't clear to me as to whether or not the information was the finding of the station or if some group of people was chanting the slogan and it was picked up by CNN and reported. What it does reveal is the fact that the information has some merit to it.

It's true that black men, especially young black men in the inner cities, quite often end up in the justice system. And so, the question is, what is the reason behind their incarceration? Are we to believe that *all* these black men who are incarcerated are innocent victims? Our objective here is to prevent young black men from getting into trouble and help them stay out of trouble. Not only that, but for them to thrive rather than just getting by. When these objectives are achieved, then and only then will these men become productive citizens in their communities.

The Need for Positive Mentors

And so, I am encouraging my reader that they should try to live a life that is beyond reproach. That is, beyond shame, beyond disgrace, and beyond rebuke. People who are engaged in wrongdoing are always looking over their shoulders! I am not sure about the feelings those people have or if they ever sleep at night. There would never be peaceful feelings knowing that law enforcement personnel were looking to find an individual. Living a life of honesty does have its rewards, as opposed to living a life of crime and violence!

The problem of domestic violence is something that one should stay away from at all cost. Many lives and homes have been ruined due to domestic violence. And so, I am warning my reader not to become a victim. Let me again stress the importance of calling on the Divine virtues within you. These virtues are patience, tolerance, willpower, and self-control. These are virtues that man was born with, and they are at your disposal 24/7.

As such, before acting on impulse, please stop and consider the consequences. Remember, the devil will tempt, but he cannot force you to do things you do not want to do!

I do not forget the problems relating to sexual crimes. Sex crimes are serious problems indeed. And no well-thinking person ever wants to be indicted on sexual charges. It's wrong to have a sexual encounter with someone without their consent. Please note that in many countries, the penalty for rape is *death*. Fortunately, in this country, this is not the case. However, the punishment for this crime in this country is very severe. And one is advised never to be involved in any form of sexual crimes.

In the case of an underage child, the punishment is even worse! And not to mention the fact that one will carry the scar around for life. Sex predator registrations and the like will be an albatross around one's neck for as long as he shall live. Rapists often receive life behind bars for raping underage children. And in my opinion, this is worse than the punishment of death. "Caution" is the keyword. One should not engage in things that one will later regret. Yes, temptations will come, but you are blessed with powers within to overcome any temptation that the enemy may throw at you!

The Need for Positive Mentors

Remember: Bring up the Child in the Way He Should Go

It should never be forgotten that quality parents will raise quality children. We often overhear the proverb "Bring up the child in the way that he should go, and when he is old he will not depart from it." Parents are the role models for their children! As a result, children imitate their parents. If the parents exhibit good and noble qualities, chances are that their children will follow in their footsteps. This is true the other way around. If parents exhibit unsavory qualities, you should expect similar quality children. Having children is one thing, but bringing up the children in the proper manner is another matter.

This brings us to the question of honesty. Children should be taught to be honest. And since all men came into this world as sinners, we are all subject to doing that which is wrong. And so, children will steal, tell untruths, and do other things of this nature. It is, however, the parents' responsibility to stamp out these things at an early age!

Since we are on this subject, I should tell you that it is not inexpensive to raise one child. It takes a tremendous amount to bring up one child—let alone two, three, four, or five children. "Put your money where your mouth is" is another saying that one should consider carefully. What this proverb is making reference to, among other things, is the fact that one should live within one's means. For example, if you are earning, let's say, $1,500 monthly, how are you spending $2,000 per month? Where will the additional $500 come from for you to stay on budget? This equally applies to the financial aspect of children. If you cannot afford to take care of one child, why bring two, three, or four children into the world?

Where will the funds come from to support them, Government assistance? Well, even in sexual matter self-control and awareness of consequences are key factor in the equation and should be observed. Indeed, there are consequences to everything and sexual matters is no exception. And so, controlling oneself and take precaution should be observed. In this case, bringing children into the world should be by design, by choice, and not by chance or accident.

Before we continue, please let me once again make it very

The Need for Positive Mentors

clear that we are not trying to disparaged our black American people! Instead, we are presenting the reader with information that will be useful to young, inner-city black men, at the lower socioeconomic level and also those who are below it. As a result, it's important to bring to attention the truth—and nothing but the truth. As such, the information in the book is not intended to be offensive to anyone! The fact is that those who are lagging behind are in need of a strong dose of truth. Therefore, I intend to bring the truth to light, no matter what! We intend to bring to their attention information that is useful in many ways. To point these people in the right and proper direction that they should go!

The Problems of Sexual Promiscuity

The problems of sexual promiscuity in the inner cities by poor, young black men in this country are cause for concerns. And yet no one seems to care about addressing the issue. Well, I intend to address it, hoping that I can make a difference in a positive manner.

Before we continue, however, please let me bring to your attention a disturbing statistic from the state of North Carolina in terms of public health issues. The report revealed that more than 17,000, about .01% percent of blacks in the state are infected with the HIV virus. Wow. This is certainly not good news! The question is, what is the reason behind this? Remember, we aren't talking about some third-world nation here. No, we are talking about the United States of America. Who is to blame? The answer to the question is plain and simple: ignorance. This is followed by poverty. What can be done to prevent a continuation? The way to stamp this out is through education!

We will get back to this in a moment, but before we do, let's consider in our imaginations seeing and admiring a beautiful black woman, and eventually falling in love. The question is, is she contaminated with a sexually transmitted disease? There is no way to tell apart from medical intervention. And so, going to bed with the woman will surely be at your peril, since she may or may not be aware that she is carrying the virus.

Now, many young, inner-city black men and women probably aren't thinking about the disease factors in the first place. And

The Need for Positive Mentors

so they engage in sexual activities without thinking about the consequences. And before you know it, both of them will come down with the HIV virus. That is, one will infect the other.

And so it's clear that many of our young men at the lower economic level seem to be out of control in terms of their sexuality. They go around having unprotected sex and impregnating young girls without any consideration whatsoever. Well, these girls are equally guilty as well. Remember, "It takes two to tango," as they say. And we must put a stop to these things ASAP. We must prove to the world that black society is in control, at least in terms of its sexuality. We cannot continue down this path and expect to gain respect. And so, changes are long overdue. Therefore, here is the proper course of action.

Whenever a boy becomes of age, he will quite naturally have the urge for sex. He should then find someone he loves, and he should get married to that person. Please note that a sexual relationship is reserved for marriage! Having unprotected sexual relations with different partners is a prescription for disaster—first, the children born out of wedlock, then the child support, and everything else in between.

Now, no man wants to see—or *should* not want to see—his sister or his mother having children with men who cannot support her children. Nor seeing her having children with multiple fathers. And what you don't want for yourself, you should not do to others. A man should not engage in sexual relationships with multiple women just for sexual pleasures. I hope that I have made this point crystal clear to my reader and to everyone in this country who is engaged is this sort of behavior.

Please note that we have placed the burden of promiscuity on the masculine gender for a good reason. You see, men are considered to be the aggressors for the most part while women are considered victims. You may be asking, "Are you sure about that?" Well, consider this: More than 99 percent of all rape cases are committed by men! And this statistic speaks for itself.

The belief that young, inner-city black men are only interested in drugs and sex seems to have some merit. Therefore, we as black people must see to it that our young black men learn to be upright men. They will be the ones who will be responsible

The Need for Positive Mentors

for producing the next generation of black people. As a result, we should see to it that they are properly equipped with the necessary skills in terms of behavior so that they will be able to function satisfactorily. This includes providing for their families and themselves.

Now, since we are on this subject, please let me tell you a true story. There was a professional black woman being interviewed on the popular *Family Feud* television show some time ago. She was a very beautiful woman. However, she was unmarried. The host of the program asked the question, "Why is it that a beautiful, professional woman like you is not married? What's going on here?" Her answer: "Well, I cannot find someone suitable, and those that I am interested in are all already taken."

My question is, where are all the young, professional black men? Please note that those who are in jail aren't professionals in the first place. And most young professionals in the suburbs are already married, as stated by the woman in question.

Are we to import young, professional black men for our professional black women? Or should we clean up and polish our young, inner-city black men for our professional black women? These are the questions before the black society in this country today.

Meanwhile, many young blacks are caught up in street gangs and have found themselves in situations many won't emerge from alive.

The Movement of Young Blacks in Street Gangs

All across this country, there are streets gang colonies, which are heavily supported by young black men. And once initiated in the movement, there is no way out except by the undertakers. And so the question is, what are the objectives of the street gang movements? In other words, what are they trying to achieve?

As far as I know, the objectives of the movement are the trafficking of narcotics, the sale of narcotics, and the distributions of weapons. During the process, members of the terrorist groups will steal from others and take others' lives, whether or not it becomes necessary.

The Need for Positive Mentors

The truth is, though, this inner-city street gang problem cuts across all racial, color, and ethnic lines! In any case, what we are concerned about here is the impact these problems have on black America and its people. This is particularly true in the case of young black men in the inner cities and towns across the nation.

These dumb fellows will not think twice about robbing and killing anyone they perceived is standing in their way, real or imaginary. They are hardened criminals in the truest sense of the words. In fact, they are a disgrace not only to themselves but to an entire race of people! And frankly, I am embarrassed whenever there are news flashes reporting robberies committed by young black men associated with street gang activities or otherwise. And I can imagine the impact of the disgrace that is brought to bear on the relatives of the robbers, not to mention the embarrassment to black people everywhere.

Now, what can black America do about these losers? We will address this in a moment, but first, let's ask a pertinent question. Why did these young black men end up in street gang activities in the first place? The reason varies. However, poverty is the root cause behind the phenomenon. Fathers not being present in their lives is a contributing factor. Also, they aren't properly educated or trained, and so ignorance has taken its course.

There are exceptions to every rule, as you are aware; however, the above-mentioned are true for the most part. I frankly believe that if these fellows were brought up in a stable, average, or above-average home environment, there would have been no reason for them to turn to a life of crime. And this is a losing situation for everyone—the parents, the individuals, and the society! And so, those young men who are engaged in street gang activities need to be educated and trained. It's doubtful, though, as to whether or not this will ever happen unless there is the willingness on their part to change. That is, the willingness on the part of those who are in the movements in the first place.

And so, I am encouraging my readers that they should stay away from the gangs. God forbid, I encourage those who happen to be in the movement to please get out of it ASAP. Remember, they aren't bringing disgrace and destruction to themselves alone but also on the race as well.

The Need for Positive Mentors

Poverty and ignorance are a dangerous combination! And as a race of people, we can do without both of them. If we eliminate the ignorance part first, the elimination of the latter will take care of itself. This is the reason I cannot overstress the importance of an education. And this should be followed by at least one marketable skill. This has been brought to your attention in past chapters, and so there is no need to go over this subject again.

In closing this chapter, you should understand that "the Lord helps those who help themselves." Remember, you were given a mind to use, and you should use it well. Sitting by with no ambition to succeed will yield no result! And so, the wise and prudent course of action is to draft a plan for success, then work on your plan until success arrives.

In this chapter, we presented information that you should put into practice.

The need for more positive role models in the inner cities was the topic of the lesson. And the question of living a life that is above reproach was also discussed. Children are supposed to be important assets. As such, they should be brought up in the proper way that they should go, and when they are old, they will not depart from it; this was also brought to your attention. Lastly, the problems of inner-city street gang violence by young black men were discussed.

In the next chapter, the question of lifting oneself up by the bootstraps will be discussed.

Chapter Seven
Let's Lift Ourselves up by the Bootstraps

As you're already aware, one of Jamaican-born Marcus Garvey's objectives was black self-reliance. And self-reliance comprises many factors, including but not limited to lifting up oneself by the bootstraps. The fact is that if black America should come of age in terms of self-sufficiency, they should not wait for manna to fall from the skies; it will not happen!

Now, before we continue, let's set the record straight, please. As we mentioned in previous chapters, black America society is divided into three categories: There are the rich, the middle-class, and the poor. By "poor" we are referring to those who are at the poverty line and below it.

The majority of blacks are at the poverty line, and many are below it!

The problem is that the poor are in need of help. And so, this is the segment of black American society that we are concerned with throughout the book! If we can lift up those at the poverty level and below it, black society will be well on its way to economic prosperity! And this is the objective that we are hoping to achieve by empowering these people who are left behind in the inner city across the United States .

Indeed, there are opportunities in the United States, many

Let's Lift Ourselves up by the Bootstraps

opportunities. This is the reason that there are people from across the globe seeking to come to this country. And many of them came only with the clothes on their backs. However, they came with the will and the desire to make something of themselves. They worked, they studied, and they put their money where their mouths were, as they say. And before you know it, they were prospering. These people see the opportunities, and they make use of them. And no one can dispute this. Many pay their taxes and are contributing in meaningful ways.

The question is, why it is that our black friends, those at the poverty line, aren't able to see opportunities? It's true that many of them aren't prepared. And as a result, they continue the status quo. The fact is that these people must lift themselves up. They should be told that no one is going to lift them up but themselves. No, no manna is not going to fall into their laps. I hate to use this analogy, but this is the truth! And they need to be told the truth. How will they progress without some form of encouragement?

One way to gain economic independence is by qualifying oneself. And one way to qualify oneself is by attending some technical school or college to acquire a skill. There are all sorts of opportunities out there! And I will go through many of them with you in a moment.

Enrolling in a Technical School

And now we come to the point where we must decide where we want to go from here. Before we do, please let me ask a question. What sort of skills do you currently possess? Or what kinds of skills would you like to acquire? If you don't have a skill, I would like to talk to you. "Skilled craftsmen are needed in all categories." Those words are commonly seen posted by corporations hold jobs fair in cities and towns across the nation. "And those who are qualified are encouraged to apply; we are an equal opportunity employer."

Unfortunately, very few if any young black men from the inner cities or towns ever show their presence at those jobs fairs. Question: Is this encouraging to black America's society? No, not at all. And so the question is, how can we change this situation? Well, I am going to lay out the foundation to be followed by all

Let's Lift Ourselves up by the Bootstraps

inner-city black men who are desirous of pulling themselves up by their bootstraps. This method is uncomplicated, regardless of whether or not one is currently employed.

Now, the first thing that one should do is find out what kind of skill one would like to pursue. When this is clear in the mind, then the hardest part is accomplished! The second path is not difficult. All one has to do is go to the community college or technical school in one's city and talk with the program director of that institution, making known your desire to attend classes and learn your skill of choice. I am sure your director will be glad to share the ins and outs of his program, the duration, and what it will cost.

Please note that if you are working, this is also possible. Going to work in the day and attending classes in the evening is a normal practice for many who desire to improve their lots in life. I myself am a product of this dynamic. And after acquiring the skill that you are interested in, there are jobs out there waiting for you! You may prefer to do your own business, and that's okay. In any case, the ball is in your court for success!

There are millions of automobiles on the roads throughout this country. And the need exists for skilled auto mechanics. But this is not all. There are millions of appliances in homes all over American. And the needs for home appliance repair technicians is enormous. There are also skilled craftsmen needed in industries, commerce and the medical fields. Broken equipment must be repaired! In addition, preventative maintenance must be carried out on working equipment. As a result, manufacturers and retailers are constantly seeking skilled technicians. In most cases, they often train technicians to specialized in servicing their products.

Next, I will tell you the manner in which you should conduct yourself in the workplace.

Behavior in the Workplace

Now, in this country and in many other civilized countries, a standard of behavior and conduct is expected of all employees who are employed in the commercial sectors, manufacturing sectors, medical fields, etc. And so, for anyone who has never

Let's Lift Ourselves up by the Bootstraps

been an employee before, there are some things that you should be aware of. If you are currently employed or were previously employed, you are aware of your company or employer's policies as they relate to rules, regulations, and conduct.

First, it should be understood that people who have been hired for the first time by most organizations are often required to serve a probationary period of time. During these probationary periods, you are being watched very carefully. And please note that one can be terminated for any reason or reasons during these periods of time. If you happen to make it past this probationary period, you will probably become a permanent member of their staff.

Note further, although you probably are now a permanent member, you will still be scrutinized from time to time. In fact, there will be files kept in connection with your performance! And so you should not knowingly break the company's rules under any circumstance. If you have any questions or concerns, you should ask your supervisor! It's a fact that anyone you may work for will not tolerate any forms of untidiness, so you should be neat, upright, and trustworthy.

In addition, you should be punctual. That is, you should be on time. If you should happen to have an emergency and cannot come to work on time, you should call in and explain to your supervisor. And above all, do not steal from your employer. I emphasize the importance of honesty to all my young, inner-city, black readers, and this is important.

Dishonesty often is a cause for instant dismissal and even prosecution. If you are honest, upright, and productive, you will probably find favor with the organization for which you are working! And so these are some of the things that you should keep in mind when you gain employment with any company, organization, or individual.

Have you ever heard about the "sting test"? It is a good thing for you to be aware of. The "honesty" or "sting test" is presented in the article below.

Let's Lift Ourselves up by the Bootstraps

The Sting or Honesty Test

Please note that there are many ways to find out whether or not a potential employee is honest. One often hears about the FBI setting up "sting" operations and to catch people engaging in criminal activities. Sting operations are not only carried out by law enforcement but by private people as well. The honesty test or sting can be carried out in the home, workplace, etc. There is no limit as to where this can be carried out! And so, the thing to remember is that you should not take things that don't belong to you. Honesty is still the best policy! Now, if you would like to find out whether or not a person is honest, you may put it to the test.

Let's use the hypothetical name Tom in our example. Let's invite Tom over to your house. But before he comes, you set up a sting to see if Tom is honest. You leave some money—ten, twenty, or thirty dollars—in a place where Tom will be. When Tom leaves your house, if the money is missing, you will have your proof that he is indeed dishonest.

Another example: Suppose I invite you to my house. Only you and I are there, and we are sitting in the living room. Beforehand, I put a denomination a twenty-dollar bill someplace on the couch. And when you leave, I find that the money has disappeared. Who should I believe has taken my money? It's you. Yes, you! You did not pass the honesty test, did you? This is only one example, but there are many other ways in which honesty/sting tests can be carried out.

In addition, there are video cameras that are often placed at various locations in order to catch dishonest people. And so, please be warned. Honesty is the best policy. In the examples, you have two choices: (1) You may choose to call the attention to the owner of the supposedly mislaid money, or (2) you can choose to pretend that you didn't see the money in the first place. Taking the money is not an option!

Note further that sting operations don't necessarily have to be money alone. It could well be jewelry, clothes, etc. And so, please be on your guard at the workplace or any other places for that matter! , We hope that you are aware of the consequences of dishonesty.

Let's Lift Ourselves up by the Bootstraps

Well, let's move on and bring some unbelievable statistics to your attention—statistics related to poverty and crime in the inner cities and towns across this nation.

Statistics Relative to Poverty, Crime, and Violence

Currently, things are not going well for young black men and black women at the lower economic level in the inner cities and towns across this nation. And heaven knows that I am doing all that I can to turn this around. The question is, where are the rich and influential black people? Why are they silent? Why are they not coming to the rescue of their people—not necessarily from a financial point of view but from a moral and intellectuals point of view? It's clear that there is a problem. And we will get to the bottom of this!

In any case, statistics have revealed that the absence of a father figure from the life of a child and a mother who falls victim to the addiction of narcotics are accountable for a sharp increase in neglected children from the age of twelve months and over. Statistics further reveal that a child who was neglected is more likely to digress rather than progress as a young adult. This raises the question in terms of crime and violence as it applies to young, inner-city black men. Heaven knows that black communities have the lion's share of this sort of ongoing predicament and these things must come to an end.

The bar must be raised to lift inner-city black communities to a higher level.

The United States is a first-rate nation. A developed nation, if you will. And so the question is, why in the world are these problems allowed to continue without abating? It is said that morality cannot be legislated. However, producing children and not being able to care for them is a decline of morality. And this should be legislated. When these things are allowed to happen, the results are problematic, and everyone can do without these stigmas. Where are the fathers of these children, anyway? As far as I am aware, its takes two people to produce a child, a female and a male. In any event, the problem of this single parent dynamics can be resolved through early childhood education. And unless this is instituted, we will continue to reap the reward

Let's Lift Ourselves up by the Bootstraps

of neglected children in society. It's clear that the powers that be aren't concerned about America's inner cities indigent situations. And so, black America should do this for themselves. And frankly, as a race of people, we can do better. And we must do better.

Statistics on Incarceration

Another serious problem in this series that we should look at and address is the problem of incarceration of young, inner-city black men. The problem of young adults getting themselves into trouble with the law is cause for concern to everyone. Black American society must find a solution for preventing our young black men from wasting their time and lives in jail. This vicious cycle (in and out of jail) must be broken, and I am making my contribution to this cause. The question is, are these young men in jail because they are innocent? Probably not. The crime probably was committed for them to have been incarcerated in the first place. And so the criticism that our young black men are being unfairly targeted by law enforcement may not be justified. What we should be doing instead is mentoring them, motivating them, and teaching them to stay out of trouble.

Recent statistics have shown that the populations of black Americans are about 12 percent. Yet, the prison populations of young black men are over 44 percent. How can this be justified? Well, I believe that they are there for good reasons and that the problems are directly linked to two dynamics: illiteracy and poverty.

The fact is that illiteracy is the major culprit behind these dynamics. When one is deprived of an education, the propensity is often for violence. And so the lack of a formal education will undoubtedly produce ignorance. This will inevitably lead to all sorts of violence and lawlessness; this is precisely what we are facing today in the inner-city black neighborhoods in this country. The record goes on to reveal that the high school dropout rate nationwide is just over 50 percent—that is, among those who have made it to high school in the first place. In the city of Baltimore, the problem is even worse. The dropout rate is said to be just over 70 percent. Now, I have no knowledge as to the cost of keeping an individual in prison as opposed to educating that individual. However, it would appear to make economic sense to educate the

Let's Lift Ourselves up by the Bootstraps

individual rather than to keep him in confinement in prison. And so, I strongly suggest that between the federal, state, and county governments, that a way should be found to educate our people, whether in prison or out.

It is said that America hasn't accepted any responsibility for racism, bigotry, and the economic disparity it has created. For example, if a white man is caught with marijuana, he will probably be given probation, rehabilitation, or warnings. On the other hand, black men are thrown in jail for committing similar crimes. As such, thousands of black men have been charged with felonies for the possession of marijuana. The fact is that this eliminates their opportunities to get well-paying jobs, financial aid for college, etc. As a result, these black men are unable to provide for their families. And they usually end up back in jail or leave their families because of the embarrassment of not being able to provide for their families.

What can be done to change these things? Will lawmakers go back to the drawing board and change the status quo? Are there two standards of justice in America?

Well, if the wrath of an offended God comes down on America, we the American people will have ourselves to blame.

In addition to ignorance, we are losing our young black men at an alarming rate to crimes and violence. It is said that homicide is the leading cause of death to young black men in the inner cities across this country. More young black men from the age of thirteen to thirty-five years of age are dying violently in the inner cities from violence than by any other cause combined, the report stated. The fact is that poverty has its negative effect on every American, whether directly or indirectly! Therefore, education is a major solution to the problem in terms of preventing poverty that inevitably leads to crime and violence.

At the beginning of this chapter, I was monitoring the civil unrest taking place in the state of Baltimore, Maryland. The problem was that a young black man lost his life while he was in the custody of the Baltimore Police. This naturally raises tensions among the black populations within the city. This unrest reaches a point that civil disobedience turns into full-scale rioting. There was burning and looting of properties. And many police officers

Let's Lift Ourselves up by the Bootstraps

sustained injuries during the riots. Resulting from the robberies and destruction of properties, many of those participating were arrested and taken to jail.

I raised this issue to make a point. Those who were involved in the destruction and lootings in their neighborhood are to be ashamed of themselves! The question is, where will they go to get goods and services? They robbed and burned groceries, pharmacies, medical clinics, etc. Will these businesses that were destroyed ever be rebuilt? Who will incline to go and do business in any communities that are apt to be destroyed due to rioting?

This sort of destruction of properties and looting that took place in Baltimore in April 2015 is not an isolated incident. These things have happened in many cities and towns in this country quite frequently. And worse, these things are almost always committed by the people living in these neighborhoods. Who on earth will be willing to go into these black neighborhoods and invest in businesses, one cannot say.

It is far more than foolish to destroy one's neighborhoods! Those who are employed are out of work. And businesses folded their tents and fled, leaving behind more economic disasters. Where are the black leaders? Where are the black rich, the black middle class, and the black influentials? Why aren't they offering any motivational assistance? It should be noted that black problems aren't white people's problems. If this were the case, these problems would have been long resolved!

Yes, white America is indebted to the black American people. But it's clear that they aren't intending to make good on their obligations to those whose ancestors did so much for this nation in terms of labor without rewards . . .

It is hopeful that things will change. And with this book in the hands of those at the lower socioeconomic level, it will change. So please, help us, God, to apply ourselves unto wisdom.

A New Beginning of Autonomy

It is hoped that this book will be the catalyst for a new dawn in black America! The intention is that this book will bring about the necessary changes for a new era in terms of changes

Let's Lift Ourselves up by the Bootstraps

for the better in every area of life in black American society. We have brought to the attention of the reader the things that we are capable of achieving.

Please note that illegal narcotics are destructive, and we must get rid of any and all trace that may be in any of our black communities. The ingestion of the poison of illegal drugs has, for too long, been destroying our people. And so, the time has come to break free from this destructive behavior for the good of black American society. Selling illegal drugs to our children and young adults will destroy their minds. And destroying black people's minds will bring further disgrace to black American society. In fact, the general conception is that inner-city young black men are dumb. Is this conception factual? Well, there are some dumb one out there for shore. However, as already mentioned, poverty doesn't necessarily equate to stupidity! And there are smart inner cities kids. They are only in need of education and training.

We can do better. And we are going to do better by cleaning up our neighborhoods and ourselves so as to be successful and upright citizens from now on and forever.

We hope that you have found this chapter interesting. Lifting oneself up by the bootstraps was the subject discussed. The manner in which one should go about acquiring a skill was discussed. In addition, the standard behavioral requirements at the workplace were presented to you. Statistics bringing to light the obstacles facing young black men were also brought to your attention. You are therefore encouraged to read the chapters over and, for Heaven's sake, please put into practice the instruction given to you.

We will continue our history discussion in the next chapter. We will give you a fundamental history lesson as it relates to black people in places such as Europe and Mexico, and I believe you will find it to be fascinating.

Chapter Eight
European and Mexican Negroes' Connection

Unless one has a thorough or even fundamental understanding of history—and in this case your history, the black history—things will pass over one's head, leaving many unanswered questions. For example, blacks who aren't aware of the history of their race are completely lacking in this knowledge. And so, if you aren't aware of the history of blacks in places such as Portugal, Spain, and Mexico, you will be mystified. Yes, there are members of the Negro race in countries such as the above-mentioned. And in this chapter, we will continue the history of black people in these parts of the world.

You have already read the histories of blacks in places such as Haiti, Cuba, Jamaica, etc. And now we will conclude with European and Mexican black history. In addition, the history of the arrival of Columbus in the New World will be presented. But first, it should be noted that before the arrival of Columbus in the Americas, Indians were the natives throughout the regions.

It is said and generally believed that we are living in a small world, and indeed, we really are. And with the advance of science and technology in terms of communication, information can be beamed anywhere around the globe, not in days, hours, or even minutes, but in seconds or milliseconds.

European and Mexican Negroes' Connection

In the old days, sending and receiving information was dependent on bulky, mechanical means. Sending international information would take months at best in comparison to today's rapid transfer of information. This is also true in relation to long-distance travel on land and also transcontinental voyages. Seamen, for example, were considered brave souls to have sailed the oceans in search of distant countries and people. People such as Christopher Columbus and others were considered to be heroes for sailing from Spain to the Americas and the Caribbean Islands. In any event, the arrival of the Spaniards in the West was considered a good omen by the Indians at first. It wouldn't be long in coming that the Indians would succumb and yield to their invaders, and so they had no choice but to surrender to them willingly at first or face the swords; the native Indians would realize that if the arrival of the outsiders, the Spaniards, was some omen, it was a bad omen for them in the long run.

Before the Spanish Arrival in Mexico

In the early days—before the internal combustion engine—sailing to distant lands on the oceans was probably adventurous and downright frightening, but there were brave men who were willing take up the challenge. And many brave souls sailed the oceans in search of finding fortunes for their countries and themselves. Christopher Columbus, for example, was one such brave man. He sailed far from Spain with the goal of finding and conquering lands and resources for his country. Antao Goncalves of Portugal, on the other hand, was engaged in similar ventures. The Portuguese seamen were vicious people.

Sailing from one country to another in the days of Columbus, Goncalves, and others took months. Months in comparison to voyages today by modern vessels that take days or weeks. Seagoing crafts in those days were dependent on the winds to propel them to distant shores in comparison to today's combustion engines. And so, yes, the world is indeed a small place, and it's getting even smaller with the invention of new technology.

Now, please let's turn our attention to the nation of Portugal and study the history of that nation as it relates to slavery in that country. Portugal is the first European nation to have enslaved black Africans.

European and Mexican Negroes' Connection

A Brief History of Slavery and the Portuguese

Everyone who is familiar with history is aware of the fact that the Portuguese sailors were the first Europeans to sail to the continent of Africa in search of treasures in the 1400s. Prince Henry of Portugal dispatched explorers to the west coast of Africa for plundering the riches there. And the Portuguese sailors not only plundered the nation's gold, diamonds, silver, ivory, etc., but they also kidnapped and forcibly took many of the natives backs to Portugal as slaves.

This is where and how it all began. They literally opened the door wide for the slave trade industries—not only to Portugal and Spain but also to the Americas, the New World. This included the Caribbean Islands and Mexico. Everyone should be cognizant of the fact that the Portuguese are the ones who first begin capturing African blacks and enslaving them in the west. In addition, they also introduced slaves to the Spanish people and in the Spanish Colonies located in the Americas and the Caribbean Islands.

And so, we see that Portugal is indeed the ringleader as far as the institution of slavery is concerned! The descendants of black slaves, wherever they are, should hold the Portuguese guilty as charged with enslaving their ancestors. They are as guilty if not more so than American slave owners. Whenever I come in contact with Portuguese, he is uncomfortable and for a very good reason! You see, many of them are familiar with black history, especially those who are from Portugal. They were taught history as it applied to black people, and this is to the credit of their educational system. Why is it that the American educational system failed to teach black history? This is the question.

Negroes in Portugal

It should never be forgotten that the Negro race comes in many different colors! However, it's not always possible at times to distinguish between those who are of the Negroid race. The important thing, though, is that the Great Intelligence that created everything designed the system in such a way that humans can intermarry and intimate with other humans with little or no consequence. This was a common practice yesterday, as it is today, and will be for the foreseeable future. This is a beautiful

European and Mexican Negroes' Connection

concept for mankind and a credit to the Supreme Creative Being. The Author has no objection to interracial marriages. After all, the brotherhood of the human race is one, regardless of the difference in colors, race, languages, or ethnic origins. This does not mean, however, that I side with the Portuguese or any others who enslaved the Africans and sexually abused them.

In 1482, Portugal's Prince Henry ordered Antonio Goncalves, Captain, to set up a trading post in Africa for trading. Goncalves, therefore, was the first to establish a European trading post on the west coast of Africa. This trading post, Fort Elmina, was established and is known today as New Guinea. Fort Elmina, therefore, was set up to trade with the Afrikaans in precious metals. However, capturing and enslaving the natives would soon take precedence over and above trading precious metals.

The Portuguese ventured far inland. They influenced the natives by presenting them with beads, mirrors, etc. In addition, the natives were given wine, whiskey, and other distilled spirits to consume, and they became intoxicated. Being under the influence, they were forcefully taken to Fort Elmina without their knowledge or without their consent. And so, being intoxicated, drunk, as they say, they could not escape their capturers.

Meanwhile, ships were waiting to transport the captives offshore. This was the beginning of the slave trafficking business in earnest. For more than 150 years, Portugal led Europe in the slave trafficking business, not only to the Americas and the Caribbean Islands but also to Spain and Portugal itself. More than 1,500 Africans were brought to Portugal annually from that time on to work in the homes and in the mines.

For centuries, blacks were part of the culture of Portugal, and they have blended in and become an integral part of the people and culture of that nation. This is also true for the Negroes in the Spanish Empire. We will take up the question of Spanish blacks later. In any case, everyone should understand that the countries that were engaged in slave trading and forced slave labor also intermingled with the female slaves. And as such, not only are the Portuguese and the Spaniards mixed with Negroes, but also the Dutch and French population as well. Portugal is located west of Spain. As such, it is the most Western country in Europe and

European and Mexican Negroes' Connection

bordered by the Atlantic Ocean.

Spanish Negroes' Connection

This brings us to the history of Spain and its Negroes' connection. The history of Spain is a long and bloody one, and I will not bore the reader by bringing the long and bitter history of Spain to light. However, it would be pertinent to bring to light the fact that Spain had been captured and conquered by many nations, including but not limited to the Roman Empire, followed by Germanic tribes after the fall of Roman, and later, the Moors from North Africa, who built a flourishing Muslim civilization. However, the Spaniards eventually drove them out of Spain.

The Portuguese people supplied the Spanish Empire with many African slaves during the time that the slaves were being brought into Portugal. And so, the slaves worked in the homes and on the farms in Spain and eventually blended in and became an integral part of Spanish culture. Today, one would be hard-pressed to distinguish between those who are mixed with Negroes.

Negroes, therefore, come in many and various hues of colors. The Negroes' Spanish background does not end in Spain! As the reader is aware, the Negroes' Spanish background can be found all over Central and South America as well as the Caribbean Islands. Please, let's give you a little history on the arrival of Christopher Columbus in the west—the Americas.

Columbus's Voyages to the West

Christopher Columbus sailed from Spain with three ships that accompanied the expedition. They were the *Nina*, the *Pinta*, and the *Santa Maria*. Many of the Portuguese and Spanish-mixed Negroes sailed with Columbus to the so-called New World, the Americas and the Caribbean Islands. People such as Balboa, De Soto, Pizarro, Mendez and others accompanied Columbus on the journey. Columbus and his entourage discovered the Caribbean Island of Haiti in 1492 and claimed it for Spain, but Spain lost it to France in 1493. And so, Haiti was the first European colony in the Caribbean.

The Haitians demanded their independent from France and

European and Mexican Negroes' Connection

became an independent nation in 1804. Haiti then became the first black republic in the West. Haiti received no economic or other assistance from France. And as such, Haiti is one of the poorest nations in the Caribbean and the Western Hemisphere.

To this day, the people of Haiti are still struggling to survive! Haiti is so poor that its people are escaping on a massive scale to the United States on whatever will float on water—thirty-two-gallon drums, inflatable inner tubes, and the like. Arriving in America, they are given the cold shoulder, not by the establishment but also by their fellow blacks as well. And so, when you come in contact with someone from the nation of Haiti, you will have a better understanding of his plight.

Christopher Columbus and his entourage went on to discover and conquer many other islands in the Caribbean region. They also discovered and conquered many South America nations, which includes but is not limited to Mexico. ,

This brings us to blacks in Mexico and their history.

Mexicans' Black Connections

Many tribes of Indians inhabited and ruled Mexico long before the arrival of Columbus and his entourage. The last ruling tribe to fall to the Spanish invasion were the Aztecs; this was in the year 1521. From that period until just over 300 years later, the Spaniards dominated Mexico, and they plundered the nation's wealth. The nation's wealth was sent to Spain while the Indians were kept poor and uneducated. Around the same period, Spain dispatched African slaves to Mexico to work on the plantations; thus, the arrival of the Negroes in Mexico. The African blacks blended in and become an internal part of Mexican culture and society.

During the Spanish inquisition of Mexico, a third group of Mexicans, "Mestizos," emerged. These "Mestizos" were a mixed race of people mostly of Indian and Spanish ancestry, *thus the term mestizos.* And so, the overwhelming number of Mexicans is of mixed ancestry. However, there are also unmixed Indians, unmixed backs, and unmixed white Spaniards in Mexico. However, the minority of white Spaniards are the ruling class in that country to this day while the overwhelming number of Mexicans

European and Mexican Negroes' Connection

are living well below the poverty line. This white Spaniard ruling class is wealthy and controls the wealth of Mexico. And because of this injustice, poor Mexicans are fleeing to the United States for better lives while the wealth of the nation ends up into the hands of the white minority.

The Mexican people overthrew Spanish domination in an uprising in 1820. However, in 1910, a nationwide revolution broke out against the injustice and the oppression of the Spaniards, and a long and bitter struggle for justice and economic participation began. During the uprising, the government confiscated large areas of privately owned farmland and divieded them up among thousands of peasants. The confiscation of lands from wealthy Spaniards to the peasants was designed to appease the rioting people and bring about some sense of calm in the country.

Mexican Gang Problems in America

There is rampant Mexican gang activity taking place here in the United States! But this is not all. There are also street gang members from other Central and South American nations here in America. They are engaged in the trafficking and sales of contraband narcotics from coast to coast, and they are the main offenders spoiling black American society, especially inner-city impoverished communities, with a wide range of illegal drugs.

The open border policy with Mexico poses a security problem for this nation and its people, and unless this problem is resolved, our nation will continue to be at the mercy of illegal activities by these people! This hits black communities in the inner cities and towns across the nation especially hard. And so, the question of crime and violence as they relate to Mexican gangsters has reached an alarming proportion. They are actually taking over the streets, and as a result, crime and violence by these hoodlums are on the rise. Recently, a Tennessee Highway patrol officer intercepted two men on Highway 40. They were pulled over by the officer. One of them did not hesitate; he pulled a revolver and shot the officer dead right there on the spot. These men were later taken into custody and were identified as two Mexicans living in the state of Texas. These men were transporting the usual marijuana to outlets in Nashville, Tennessee.

European and Mexican Negroes' Connection

This killing is not an isolated incident! It is an ongoing phenomenon that is taking place from Boston to Las Angeles and every state between. The street gang problem regarding illegal aliens and also many legal residents poses a serious problem in the United States, and this cannot be allowed to continue. In East Los Angeles, California for example, the Mexican gangs rule supreme. Their activities aren't restricted to California alone; they are growing in numbers and are running rampant all across this country. And because of their willingness to rain terror on this country, murdering by the brotherhood has skyrocketed wherever they dominate. They are a force to be reckoned with, and even the police seem to be intimidated by these hoodlums.

There are at least three separate and distinct known Mexican gangs operating in the United States with tens of thousands of members. In California, they are slowly but surely taking over South Central Los Angeles. This area is a stronghold for inner-city black Americans in Los Angeles. The question is, when are the American people going to cry "we've had enough"? Are the police powerless to put an end to these thugs? If so, where is our army, our air force, and out marines?

Recently, I was watching a documentary on a popular television channel on the question of gang activities in the state of California. One member from a Mexican gang was being interviewed, and one from the Crips was also being interviewed. The Mexican gang member admitted, "We are there to protect our turf and to keep intruders out." He went on to admit, "If anyone comes into our neighborhood without good reason, they will be killed. We are here to protect each other, and our opponents are protecting their turf as well."

And so, this tit for tat goes on unabated between Mexican gangsters in East Los Angeles and black gang members in South Central Los Angles. Crossing the border into the turf of the rival could mean instant death. In fact, the reporter brought to light the fact that two high school students had been gunned down by a Mexican gang member in cold blood not long before the day of the debate. These high school students were not affiliated with any gang members. They were simple on the street in their neighborhoods playing when they were brutally slain.

European and Mexican Negroes' Connection

It was further revealed that the shooting was aimed at anyone in the black neighborhoods as revenge. The shooting was a way to bring to the attention of the rivals that they were a force to be reckoned with. And so, the reporter politely asked a black member of the Crips whether or not gang activity would ever end. His answer was a conclusive "No" to the question. He went on: "They cannot stop gang activities. If they could have, they would have stopped it twenty years ago . . . It's easier to pull all the weeds from a garden than to get rid of the gangs."

Now, is this statement correct? Are we not able to dismantle gang activities in America? These ignorant fellows—most of whom didn't even complete grammar school, let alone high school or college—are taunting the government, proclaiming that they are cleverer. Only federal, state, and county government officials can answer these questions. In any event, if they are willing to allow these gangsters, Mexicans and all, to continue dumbing down this nation with criminal activities and other violent crimes, so be it.

The recent uprisings by the American people against illegal alien activities and illegal aliens in this country are completely justified. This justification isn't based solely on the reduction of jobs and the breaking of the medical institution in terms of services without payments, but also on the dynamics of crime and violence by these illegals as well.

In addition to all of the above, the question of drunken illegals driving without a license or insurance is a cause for concern! These uninsured operators of motor vehicles pose great danger to life and prosperity. As a result of unlicensed illegal alien drivers in this country, many states are considering granting driver's licenses to illegal aliens. Many Americans believe that handing driver's licenses to illegals should not be an option. This would be synonymous to rewarding a criminal for committing a crime. In any case, our elected officials are the ones we have elected to administer the affairs of the nation, and they should come up with some sort of effective solutions to the illegal immigration problems and the open border policy with Mexico.

In this chapter, I brought to the reader's attention fundamental history as it relates to slavery and slave trafficking. In addition, the

European and Mexican Negroes' Connection

historical connections between Spanish and Portuguese blacks, as well as those in Mexico and the United States, were revealed to you. Emphasis was also placed on the voyage of Columbus and his arrival to the New World. The plights of the Mexican people were also brought to the attention. And so, I hope that you have found this to be informative.

People are often influenced positively or negatively on a constant basis! And so, in the next and final chapter, we will look at some of the negative and positive implications of influence on the human psyche.

Chapter Nine
You Should Stay Away from Bad Influence

*I*t's interesting to note that there are people who can be easily influenced and swayed by the suggestions and actions of other people! A child can be influenced by adults since they are dependent on adults for proper direction and guidance. Full-grown adults, on the other hand, are able—or should be able—to think for themselves. If an individual isn't able to think and make reasonable and rational decisions, then they are open for others to make decisions for them. And this is where many problems stem from in terms of negative influence. People are being influenced negatively, and as such, many are getting themselves into all kinds of trouble. This is the reason one should stay away from people who will influence one negatively. If you are aware that someone is leading you in the wrong direction, it is your responsibility to do one of two things: (1) shun that person straight away, or (2) ignore their suggestion completely.

Those with strong minds and willpower will not be easily influenced negatively. Whenever the tempter comes and makes bad suggestions, whatever the situations may have been, they are simply rebuffed, or they ignore the tempter completely. It is said that the devil "tempts but he doesn't force." There is wisdom behind this proclamation. Indeed, no one can make anyone do anything without one's consent. Unless, of course, one is under

You Should Stay Away from Bad Influence

the wrong influence. The question is, what do I mean by "wrong influence"? Answer: mentally deranged, under the influenced of alcohol, narcotic, even demon possessed. Any one or all of the above will in all likelihood take possession of the mind and bring about the destruction of an individual.

A sane and sound mind is in control of the body, and no one can make you do something that you object to doing! We will come back to this subject later in this chapter since you should understand that you are in total control of your actions—and no one else. As a result, you should be careful of the company you keep. You should seek company that will inspire you positively!

I have written this book so as to bring about change to black America, especially to young, inner-city blacks at the lower socioeconomic level across this nation. Young blacks who fall into the categories mentioned are at a disadvantage! And if there is no immediate and sustained change, black in America will be at a disadvantage, if they aren't already. They will gradually diminish and eventually go extinct.

As mentioned in previous chapters, my objective, therefore, is to bring about the necessary motivational encouragement to these people. To motivate inner-city blacks at the poverty level who are lagging behind, to get them qualified so as to make significant contributions to themselves, their connections, and also the society.

As a black man myself who migrated to this country, frankly, I am embarrassed to see the condition of poor blacks in America. The truth is that there is enough blame to go around. Nevertheless, self-preservation is the key. And those who are desirous of making the future bright have the duty and responsibility to prepare themselves. The manner in which to go about preparing was brought to your attention in earlier chapters! The process entails training.

Upper-class blacks, as well as middle-class black people, are more or less doing well! However, most of their counterparts in the inner cities aren't doing well at all. And so, these are the people I am trying to reach with this book. In any event, well-to-do blacks need to pool their resources in order to come to the rescue of their people who are left behind.

You Should Stay Away from Bad Influence

There are wealthy blacks who are more than able to assist blacks at the poverty line. I can think of many of them. The first thought that came to my mind is the rich lady who is a mega television personality: "the black queen of talk television." She is very rich. And besides, she is single and unmarried. She can singlehandedly send over 5,000,000 young, inner-city black men and girls to community college to gain marketable skills. In addition, what about our black athletics stars, musicians, and artists who are being fools with their fortunes, with their lavish lifestyles, spectacle weddings, expensive cars, and mansions? How can these people have good times while their brothers and sisters in the inner cities are perishing? This is beyond reasoning.

Use the Head and Not the Heart So Much

It is said by many in the upper-class structure that "the masses are naïve." And there is some truth to their belief. In the first place, we have seen the behavior of many of them constantly. Many of these people do things that defy logic. And I will bring a few of them to your attention. Not that you aren't aware of them! But I want to support the belief of those in the middle and upper class.

In the first place, many of these people seem to be incapable of holding on to their hard-earned money—those who are gainfully employed. They wasted their money on trivial and meaningless things as if there will be no tomorrow. Expensive shoes, cars, massive flat-screen televisions; the list goes on and on. Those expensive sneakers that some of those young men are wearing are incredible.

In addition, there are those who have brought children into this world before preparing for the children. The worst part is that many of these people don't stop at one or two children but three, four, or five. They failed to realize the fact that it's not inexpensive to raise children. Not if they should become outstanding citizens. Although, fortunately, many of these children does become outstanding citizens. The point is that they should be aware of the fact that unprotected intercourse often leads to pregnancy. On the other hand, people in the upper-class structure who are financially able often have one or two children. And there is a good reason for this. A person who is well off and planned to

You Should Stay Away from Bad Influence

have many children often stays home to raise their children. Or they employ a nanny to take care of the children when they go to work.

A classic case of inner-city poverty: I read in the daily newspapers sometime in November 2015 the story of a young man who was shot and killed, leaving behind five children. It appeared that this victim was a member of a notorious street gang. It's clear that this man was uneducated and had no skills. This is probably the reason he became a member of the gang in the first place. Yet he had five children that he left behind. Skill or no skill, educated or not educated, having more than one or two children is a sure way to stay in poverty as far as the poor are concerned! This is only one example. However, this can be multiplied many times. In fact, this problem is common in many poor, black communities. Well, not only in black communities but in many poor communities across this nation!

I know that this is a moral issue and that morality cannot be legislated. Nevertheless, it should be mandatory that people in this county should not be permitted to have children until they are able to care for children.

Children must be well-fed. They must be educated, well disciplined, and given some sort of marketable skills to be able to earn a decent living. And having more than one or two children will increase the likelihood of the children not having the necessary requirements to go out into the world and be winners. This is one of the many problems facing inner-city blacks and others. Not to mentioned the absence of a father figure from the equation. Children who originated from such a deprived environment are paying a hard price in this society! Unfortunately, many of these children often end up engaged in lawlessness—engaged in contraband, robbery, drugs—and, God forbid, ending up in prison or dead.

There is no one to tell them right from wrong. And many are easily influenced. If their counterparts engage them into doing things that are unlawful, they are ready to follow suit simply because they know no better! They aren't taught to stay away from bad company; there is no one to point them in the right direction. And the problem is that whenever their counterparts

You Should Stay Away from Bad Influence

get themselves into trouble, even if they themselves weren't physically engaged in taking part in a robbery, etc., since they are in company with the wrongdoers, they are also considered guilty and are often taken into custody as well.

Based on this fact, you should not associate with those who are engaged in lawlessness. You should stay clear of street gangs and their members. Remember, whenever the cops come for those who have committed the crimes, if you are in their presence, it's assumed that you are a part of it and will be taken to jail as well! And as you know, to free you from confinement is not inexpensive. Therefore, you should endeavor to use the head and not the heart. The Lord has given you, and everyone else, a head to control not only your body but your destiny as well!

Indeed, the popular belief that "the massive aren't necessarily bright" seems to be . authentic. How, then, can one explain the behavior of many at the lower strata of the society? Another example: a man went into a bank armed with a semi-automatic weapon and commanded everyone in the bank to lie on the floor. He then emptied the vaults and tried to escape. But he was surprised by a contingent of police and sheriff helicopters that were pursuing him along this escape route. The bank robber was apprehended. Now, why in the world did he believe he would escape?

And so, for the rest—who are engaging in criminal activities—why these people believe they will not be caught is beyond reason. Criminal fugitives, more often than not, are apprehended. They are always caught, sooner or later, and brought to justice. The fact is that there are many depraved souls among us. These people fail to think about the effect of their lawless actions. Crime doesn't pay! And honesty is indeed the best policy.

The problem of crime and violence is not restricted to any particular race, gender, or ethnic origin. This cuts across all boundaries in its quest to bring degradation to the human race. In fact, moral decay seems to on the rise here in this country. Things that were once looked on as outrageous and disgraceful are now being embraced with open arms. Could it be the removal of religion and religious practices from the school? Whatever the case may have been, one thing is certain. This nation is declining.

You Should Stay Away from Bad Influence

The decline is widespread and is taking its toll from coast to coast.

It's Unlawful to Aid and Abet a Fugitive

The question of "aiding and abetting fugitive" may not sound familiar to you. Nevertheless, you will have an understanding of its meaning as we continue in the article. The fact is, this aiding and abetting dynamic is a serious matter from a legal standpoint. And you should have nothing to do with the matter, ever. It is said that "ignorance of the law is no excuse." This may well be the case; however, it's unfortunate and unfair to the average person since he probably is not a legal scholar.

In truth, and in fact, in any civilized society, there are laws, rules, and regulations. They are there for the most part to protect lives and property. Knowing all the laws, ordinances and regulations is virtually impossible for those of us who aren't legal professionals. This is the reason that it's prudent for one to seek legal advice whenever necessary!

Now, if someone committed a crime and is fleeing to avoid justice, and you or anyone else knowingly or unknowingly allows that person to take cover under your roof, you are essentially aiding and abetting that person, a fugitive! Please note that such an offense is a criminal felony, and the penalty for such violation is severe. Please note further that a fugitive doesn't have to be in your house. He could be in your motor vehicle or simply in your company, wherever you are! This is the reason that you should be careful of the company you keep and the influence you are exposed to from your company. Association doesn't necessarily equate to friendship. These are two separate and distinct matters for the most part.

You should be aware of the fact that it's very easy to get into trouble! And it's not always very easy to get out of trouble. This is the reason that it's wise to be cautious. One should endeavor to seek the help of God in all one's undertaking. No one knows what the day will bring. In fact, there are those who left the house to never return safely, if at all. Many end up in jail, some at the emergency ward, while others end up at the public mortuary waiting to be identified. You should be careful of the people you "hang around with," as they say. And remember, an ounce of

You Should Stay Away from Bad Influence

prevention is worth a pound of cure!

Thou Shall Not Commit Adultery, Thou Shall Not Steal, and Thou Shall Not Kill

Those who are familiar with biblical doctrine are aware of the Ten Commandments. The Ten Commandments were given by God to Moses thousands of years ago. They were given for the preservation of man's mind, his body, and his soul. The Commandments can be found in Exodus, Chapter 20. It's not my intention to present to you the entire Ten Commandments in this chapter. You can read the Commandments for yourself.

I will present to you three Commandments from the series so as to make very important points in connection with our presentation. Before we continue, I want to pose a question to you. Are all men created equal? This question has become a whipping boy in connection with the civil rights movement. The late Dr. Martin Luther King Jr. placed great emphasis on the equality of all men dynamic.

I contemplated this philosophy for many years and came to one conclusion; I am not sure whether or not all men are created equal. Medical science, in my opinion, may not be in the possession of all the facts at its disposal so as to render a verdict on the matter one way or another. If it is possible to dialogue with the Creator of man, the question could be directed to Him. Then and only then **will the true verdict be known**. Now, to the Commandments.

Thu Shall Not Commit Adultery

This is very clear and was given by the Creator for the preservation of life and property. Staying away from committing adultery, therefore, is a wise course of action. Most of us are fully aware of the consequences often resulting from "the triangle effect" by breaking this command. This is not just the result of ruining homes and families, but also the bodily injuries that often result to those who are caught in the triangle. Even physical death often is the result of the "fallout effects" of betrayals. If you are married, you will have a better understanding of this dynamic. Unfaithfulness, betrayal, and low self-esteem are some

You Should Stay Away from Bad Influence

of the stigmas that are brought to bear on those who are on the receiving end of adultery! And this can be devastating to those who aren't able to exercise self-control, tolerance, and willpower.

Thou Shall Not Steal

This Commandment is one of those most widely abused, in my opinion. Stealing is a problem wherever you turn. It's right there, staring you smack the face! And with the advent of the Internet, the sky is the limit. There are white-collar crimes resulting from stealing, there are blue-collar crimes, and the list goes on and on and on. The good Lord knows the depravity of the human race. And so He anticipated that man would be tempted to take his brother's possessions. He then gave him specific instructions that man should not take his brother's belonging.

The fact is that stealing is a worldwide problem. People have launched all kinds of Ponzi schemes in order to steal from others! The worst of them all, however, is the robber that breaks into people's homes and forcefully steals their belongings. But this is not all. There are robbers who not only break in and steal, but they also take the life/lives of their victim(s). This act is a testament to the depravity of men. That is, men of low morals.

There are wicked people who are capable of doing very evil things. And all men are known by their deeds. Whenever a person is high on a controlled substance, it appears that the mind goes blank. As such, this person is void of common sense, reason, and the ability to make sound judgment. And, unfortunately, this is the way of life for many at the lower economic level in big cities across this nation.

You who are reading this book—I believe that you have a firm desire to be an upright individual. Am I right about this? This is the reason that you are seeking knowledge in the first place. Well, now that you are reading, I am sure that you have seen things from a different perspective. I urge you, therefore; please do not be tempted to steal. Be honest and upright. Every temptation that you have conquered you will be given more power! And remember, "**Strength for your labor, the Lord will provide.**"

You Should Stay Away from Bad Influence

Thou Shall Not Kill

Life is a precious gift indeed, from the Lord! Therefore, it is written, "Woe unto him that taketh the life of another." There will be no forgiveness for him who willfully has taken the life of his brother! He will certainly face the wrath of an offended Deity sooner or later. There are ignorant people who have shed innocent blood and aren't thinking about the consequences that will, sooner or later, come upon their heads.

It's true that one can repent of one's sin. Nevertheless, "one will still reap that which one has sown." This is a command that is inescapable, even within the grave. It makes no difference whether or not we believe in the survival of the soul in the afterlife. In fact, we cannot change the laws of nature. And so we should accept things for what they are.

Now, from a biblical, doctrinal standpoint, the first slaying that was recorded was the slaying of Abel by his brother Cain, the two sons of Adam and Eve. This slaying brought a Divine curse on the human, lasting race to this day. The Lord commanded man that he should not take the life of his brother. Killing another human is wrong in the first place, and it is a barbaric action. And the consequence that follows suit is devastating to those who are guilty!

It should be noted in the first place **that all men are brothers**. This is based on the fact that all men originated from common biblical ancestors: Adam and Eve! Now, after the flood in the days of Noah, the earth was flooded, and all living things were destroyed except eight people. There were only eight people who survived the wrath of God by way of the flood. They were Noah, his wife, their three sons, and their wives. These are our ancient ancestors that replenished the earth after the terrible Deluge, as we know it today. Again, all men are brothers! And thou shall not kill. Therefore, this command is directed to man so that he should not kill his brother.

Taking the life of another is a sure way of bringing Divine vengeance upon our head. You see, the soul of the departed will cry out to God, his maker, and as sure as night follows day, the vengeance of the Lord will sooner or later descend on the heads of those who have taken the life of their brothers! It is written in

You Should Stay Away from Bad Influence

the Ten Commandments: "**for I the Lord thy God am a jealous God, visiting the iniquity of the fathers upon the children unto the third and fourth generation of them that hate me; and showing mercy to thousands of them that loved me, and keep my commandments**." Indeed, the sins of the father do come on his children! This is generally known as a generational curse. Therefore, to prevent the wrath of God, we had better abstain from evil.

There are unpardonable sins! One of which is the taking of life. However, there is no need for us to go into detail in this presentation. And so, you are encouraged to read the commandments to determine those that are unpardonable.

How it is that someone is aware of the consequences of taking innocent life and goes ahead and kills anyway? Or is it that they aren't aware of the consequences? Or is it that they cannot control the temper? The temper can be a barrier. The loss of the temper often results in one doing unsavory things that often brings regret.

People who have taken innocent lives, more often than not, always meet with a violent end. "He shall surely reap whatever he has sown" is a biblical statement that was made by the Messiah, Jesus the Christ. There are people who have taken the lives of others who are deeply remorseful. Many of these people are themselves often slain by others. Some of these are murders while others are suicide. Why is this? Because of guilt!

In fact, there are tormented people all around. They cannot live with themselves because of the wrongs that they have done. You see, a guilty conscience is a terrible thing! And so, I am warning you who are reading this book. Be upright. Stay clear of doing things that are offensive to others, to your race, and to the Almighty. Not to mention the vengeance of the Lord that is sure to come on your children.

As already mentioned, there are Ten Commandments! You are encouraged to read them for yourself. They can be found in Exodus, Chapter 20.

You Should Stay Away from Bad Influence

O' the Brotherhood of Men

Let's continue the presentation in connection with Noah, his wife, their sons, and their sons' wives who were saved in the Ark. It's my intention to bring to you additional information concerning the history of the replenishing of the earth after the flood. Now, the names of Noah's sons, which were saved from the destruction of the earth by the flood, were Shem, Ham, and Japheth. From these three men and their wives, the earth was replenished and is continuing to replenish to this day!

Therefore, men can be divided into three categories according to their ancestors as follows: (1) the Jews, the Persians and the Syrians, ancestors of Shem, (2) the Egyptian and the Ethiopians, descendants of Ham, and (3) the Europeans, descendants of Japheth.

From these assessorial lines, all men originated. However, due to interracial mingling and marriages, there are mixed cultures. It should be noted that mixed cultures aren't considered to be a race. There are what they are, mixed cultures. Let's take Latinos, for example. They are mostly Indians mixed with whites. This is the concept of mixed culture! Indeed, the melting pot dynamics are alive and well all over the world and certainly here in the United States. There are blacks mixed with whites, Indians mixed with blacks, the list goes on and on and on!

In terms of the origins of the human race, this history is interesting, isn't it? Adam and Eve, the first two people, created many generations before Noah and the people who lived in Noah's days. Then came the flood, and the earth was cleansed. After which, the generations of Noah continue through his descendants. And here we are today. Due to the wickedness of the people in Noah's days, the Lord sees it just to bring destruction on the earth by a flood. And so, the replenishment of the earth begins with our ancient forefathers: Shem, Ham, and Japheth. Time marches on. There were many generations after Noah. And here we are in this generation, you and I and many others. One hundred years from today, we will be "out of here," as they say. In fact, you and I probably will be long gone before then. The interesting thing is that we will meet our Maker! And we will reap our just reward or punishment—recompense!

You Should Stay Away from Bad Influence

It should be noted that everything that we have done will be brought to light. And we will be accounted for the things that we had done, or the things that we failed to do.

In closing, let me remind you, stay away from people who will influence you negatively. Refuse that which is evil and accept only that which in good and noble. And remember, the strength to resist that which is destructive, the Lord will provide!

Conclusion

Before we conclude and present the appendix, the writer would like to reiterate an important point here: Young, inner-city blacks at the poverty line and below must lift themselves up through the refinement and enlightenment of education. Those who are left behind must lift themselves up by the bootstraps.

It's clear that the powers that be have completely failed those who are deserving of the most help and are entitled to the most assistance. It's their right to an education. In addition, they should be given marketable skills. Instead, they were taught to be dependent rather than to be independent.

As a result, poor, young, inner-city black men are in danger of going extinct. This seems to have been pre-programmed into the system. And clearly, the effects are being manifested all across the nation.

And so, they have no alternative but to take their futures into their hands and do things for themselves. This is the purpose of this book: to motivate young, inner-city black men into excellence and to help them become productive citizens. They need to be shown the way out of poverty and hopelessness. And there seems to be no one willing to engage in this task, as far as I am concerned. Well, it's distressing to note that wealthy and middle-class blacks don't find it necessary to come to the aid and assistance of their less fortunate people.

Conclusion

Young, impoverished blacks in the cities and towns across this nation are in need of positive role models. Not necessarily from those who are in athletics, but from black intellectuals: scientists, engineers, and professionals in medicine, law, etc. Therefore, let's not ask what these less fortunate people can do for us but what *we* can do for our less fortunate inner-city blacks in this country, the United States of America.

Appendix

Inner-city blacks at the poverty line must prepare themselves to make use of present and future opportunities. This can be achieved by some preparations. First, those who haven't finished school should return and complete their education. Those who have finished high school are well ahead of the game. It should be noted, however, that graduating from a high school is one thing, but where does one go from there? A high school certificate is a good thing, and we commend those who have completed that journey. But this is only a stepping stone. That is, a path on a further journey.

Now, it's clear that not everyone will become a rocket scientist. Nevertheless, there are other things that one is able to accomplish functioning at the high school level. And I will attempt once again to bring these things to light. Therefore, the first thing that one should consider, in my opinion, is some form of skill or vocation. *Attending a technical school or community college to acquire a skill would be a good investment*! This should be strongly considered. Those who so desire may enter into the commercial sector. There are many high school graduates who have gained placements in offices, etc. As mentioned, however, with a high school certificate, one should pursue higher education.

Those who, unfortunately, didn't finish school should go back and finish their education, as mentioned. And after earning a high school certificate, they are encouraged to conform themselves to the instructions presented above.

Appendix

Those who are lagging behind will not meet with success. And they will always be at a disadvantage in comparison to those who are progressing. "Getting by" is not something to be proud of! Instead, one should seek to strive and prosper day after day. Fortunately, education is free up to the high school level. In addition, student loans are available for those who desire to go to college! Therefore, there is no excuse for any young black men to be lagging behind. Rise, move forward, and make your people proud. Remember, many are watching and are hoping that you fail so as to cast doubt on whether or not you are capable of accomplishing anything.

The author firmly believes that education and training, skills, are black America's most formidable weapons. And make no mistake; if you are qualified, you will get work. For example, there is an acute shortage of skills in almost all professions and trades in this country. And as such, expatriates are coming in and filling these needs while young blacks are losing out immensely. This practice must change. It can be changed, and it will be changed! The writer will not cease to instill the importance of taking control of the present so as to prepare the future until black America comes up to par with their white counterparts.

We are aware that there are unsavory elements within the black communities that are pulling down the entire race with their unsavory behaviors. Drugs, crime, and violence, and street gang activities. The reasons behind these things were brought to your attention in previous chapters. In addition, confrontations with law enforcement are taking their toll. In fact, not only with the police but with other blacks as well. Black-on-black killings are something that many blacks themselves would probably rather not talk about. In any event, the major reasons behind these things are poverty and ignorance! Once those at the lower level are uplifted, things will begin to change for the better. And to bring about changes and to instill empowerment to those who are at a disadvantage, everyone should come to the assistance of inner-city blacks. Wealthy blacks, middle-class blacks, and black intellectuals all have their parts to play in the equation.

I am hopeful that not only affluent black Americans of goodwill may lend a helping hand to their fellow Americans in the inner cities and towns who are desperately in need, but also

Appendix

white Americans of goodwill as well. We are also requesting the assistance of our brothers and sisters in the news media. They may help these young, inner-city black men by bringing the book to their attention. And they should understand that their labor will not be in vain

    Those who seek to lend a helping hand should not worry because "Strength for Their Labor, The Lord Will Provide."

About the Author

About the Author

James A. Hudson originated from Kingston, Jamaica. He then became a naturalized American citizen. James Hudson's early childhood education was in Jamaica: from preschool, primary school, high school, and at the King's Technical College. He was also educated at Roxbury College, Massachusetts and at Cal State Fullerton, California. James is an electronics technician by profession.

James Hudson's work in history goes back to the 1970s when he was an employee of the local government of the city of Kingston, Kingston and Saint Andrews Corporation. Here in the United States, James worked with the Motorola Communicants Corporation before accepting a position with the General Service Agency, GSA, as a Communication specialist in Orange County California. The General Service Agency was later dissolved, and maintenance of the Orange County Communications system was turned over to the Orange County Sheriff's Department. As a result, James was assigned to the Orange County Sheriff's Department, Sothern California as a communications specialist.

James is also an Author! He is the published author of three books, *How to Have a Better Relationship with Your Mate/Spouse*, *Thou Shall Not Kill What Providence Has in Store for Those Who Do*, and *The Rising of Black America with the Assistance of White America*.

CPSIA information can be obtained
at www.ICGtesting.com
Printed in the USA
FSHW010025090620
70734FS